GRAMMAR OF POETRY

STUDENT EDITION

IMITATION IN WRITING SERIES

Grammar of Poetry is part of the *Imitation in Writing* series, designed to teach the art and discipline of crafting delightful prose and poetry.

POETRY
Poetry Primer
Grammar of Poetry

LITERATURE
Aesop's Fables
Fairy Tales
Medieval Legends
Greek Myths
Greek Heroes

Published by Canon Press
P.O. Box 8729, Moscow, ID 83843
800.488.2034 | www.canonpress.com

Matt Whitling, *Grammar of Poetry: Student Edition*
Copyright © 2000 by Matt Whitling.
Copyright © 2012 by Canon Press.
First Edition 2000 by Logos Press
Second Edition 2012 by Canon Press
Cover design by Rachel Hoffmann.
Interior layout and design by Lucy Zoe.
Printed in the United States of America.

Grammar of Poetry: Student Edition
 ISBN-13: 978-1-59128-119-1
 ISBN-10: 1-59128-119-9

Library of Congress Cataloging-in-Publication Data

Whitling, Matt.
 Grammar of poetry : student edition / Matt Whitling. -- 2nd ed.
     p. cm. -- (Imitation in writing)
 Includes bibliographical references and index.
 Audience: Grade: 7-8.
 Previous ed.: 2000.
  ISBN 978-1-59128-119-1 (alk. paper) -- ISBN 1-59128-119-9 (alk. paper)
 1. Poetry--Authorship. 2. Creation (Literary, artistic, etc.) 3. Poetics. I. Title.
 PN1059.A9W45 2012
 808.1--dc23

14 15 16 17 18   10 9 8 7 6 5   2012026460

GRAMMAR OF POETRY
STUDENT EDITION

Matt Whitling

canonpress
Moscow, Idaho

Lovers and madmen have such seething brains,

Such shaping fantasies, that apprehend

More than cool reason ever comprehends.

The lunatic, the lover, and the poet

Are of imagination all compact:

One sees more devils than vast hell can hold—

That is the madman. The lover, all as frantic,

Sees Helen's beauty in a brow of Egypt:

The poet's eye, in a fine frenzy rolling,

Doth glance from heaven to earth, from earth to heaven;

And, as imagination bodies forth

The forms of things unknown, the poet's pen

Turns them to shapes, and gives to airy nothing

A local habitation and a name.

Such tricks hath strong imagination,

That, if it would but apprehend some joy,

It comprehends some bringer of that joy;

Or in the night, imagining some fear,

How easy is a bush supposed a bear!

—Shakespeare
A Midsummer Night's Dream

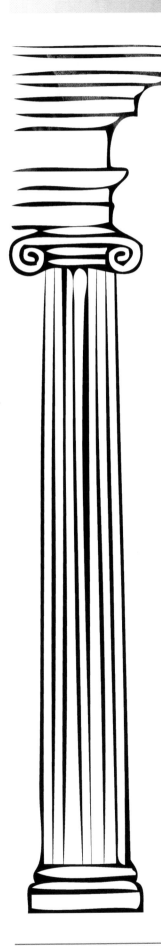

CONTENTS

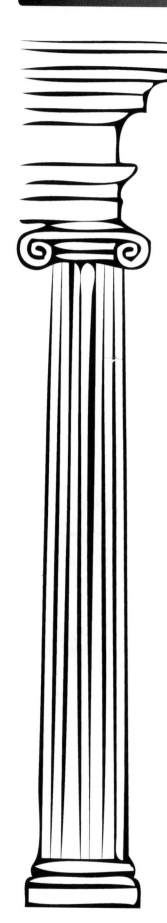

MODULE VIII: 117

MODULE IX: 135

APPENDICES   159

PREFACE

A DEFENSE OF THE CLASSICAL TOOL OF IMITATION

Scripture commands us to imitate the Lord Jesus Christ. We are also commanded to imitate those brothers and sisters who, through faith and patience, have inherited the promises. To imitate something or someone means:

- To do or try to do after the manner of; to follow the example of; to copy in action.
- To make or produce a copy or presentation of; to copy, reproduce.
- To be, become, or make oneself like; to assume the aspect or semblance of; to simulate.

This God-sanctioned method of learning is an essential tool for educating young people. Consider how we go about teaching a child to perform skills such as throwing and catching.

"Hold your hands *like this*," we say. "Step forward as you throw *like this*."
"Look at this 'A'. Trace *this letter*. Now, you try to make an 'A' like this one."

This is imitation, and it extends beyond writing. At Logos School, for example, students learn how to paint by imitating master painters of the past. "Students, this is a good painting. Let's see if you can reproduce it." Regardless of whether we are teaching music, reading, or math, imitation very often provides the best starting block in instruction in any of these areas.

Educators in seventeenth century England valued imitation as a tool to teach style, particularly in the area of writing. These English grammar schools primarily employed a method of imitation called the Double Translation.

Consider these steps that were used in a Double Translation after the teacher translated a Latin work into English:

1. The student copied the English translation over paying close attention to every word and its significance.
2. The student wrote the English and Latin together one above the other making each language answer to the other.
3. The student translated the original Latin to English on his own. (This was part one of the Double Translation).
4. Ten days later the student was given his final English translation and required to turn it back into good Latin.

Benjamin Franklin wrote of a similar exercise that he employed to educate himself a century later. As a young man, he came across a particular piece of writing that he delighted in, *The Spectator*, a series of 555 popular essays published in 1711 and 1712. These essays were intended to improve manners and morals, raise the cultural level of the middle-class reader, and popularize serious ideas in science and philosophy. These well written essays contained a style Franklin felt eager to emulate. Here Franklin explains his method of "double translation" regarding The Spectator:

"With the view (imitating this great work) I took some of the papers, and making short hints of the sentiments in each sentence, laid them by a few days, and when, without looking at the book, tried to complete these papers again, by expressing each hinted sentiment at length, and as fully as it had been expressed before, in any suitable words that should occur to me. Then I compared my Spectator with the original, discovered some of my faults, and corrected them."

He became aware of his need for a greater stock of words in order to add variety and clarity of thought to his writing.

"Therefore I took some of the tales in the Spectator, and turned them into verse; and, after a time, when I had pretty well forgotten the prose, turned them back again. I also sometimes jumbled my collection of hints into confusion, and after some weeks endeavored to reduce them into the best order, before I began to form the sentences and complete the subject. This was to teach me method in the arrangement of thoughts. By comparing my work with the original, I discovered many faults and corrected them; but I sometimes had the pleasure to fancy that, in particulars of small consequence, I had been fortunate enough to improve the method or the language, and this encouraged me to think that I might in time become to be a tolerable English writer, of which I was extremely ambitious."

This Imitation In Writing series seeks to provide instruction in writing using the classical tool of imitation. As we begin imitation in poetry, we will employ a similar method to what Franklin described. We will find poems of truth, beauty, and goodness and emulate them, and maybe if we're diligent, we might in time become tolerable writers, too.

LESSON ONE

INTRODUCTION

POETRY
is a language
of pictures
and music.

TROPE
is a
specific fig-
ure of speech.

The music of poetry
contains two parts
METER & RHYME.

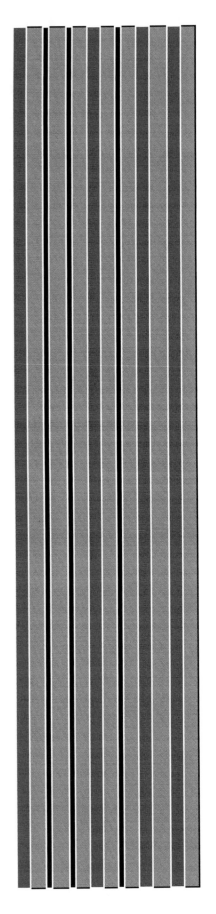

This book consists of nine modules. In each module we will typically study one trope, one element of meter, and then do an imitation. This will give you the opportunity to master each poetic element as you add to your knowledge incrementally.

WHAT IS POETRY?

Although poetry can be defined in many different ways, for our purposes, we will define poetry as a language of pictures and music. A good writer paints pictures with his words in figurative language. A specific figure of speech is called a **trope**. Think of tropes as the pictures poets paint with words. Poetry uses meter as the music presenting the pictures. The music of poetry contains two parts: **meter** and **rhyme**. Meter and rhyme combine to produce the lilting sound and rhythm that most poems contain.

EPIPHANY CHART

In order to write a good poem, you will need to have a meaningful topic to write about. The epiphany chart will help you organize your topics. The word epiphany means to "show" or "reveal." By completing the chart, you will be listing items that show or reveal something significant about you.

In the columns on the next page, fill each section with as many ideas as you can:

- **High Points** – the best things that have ever happened to you (success, honor, happiness, etc.)

- **Low Points** – the worst things that have ever happened to you (injuries, failures, embarrassing moments, etc.)

- **Turning Points** – events that have changed you in some way (a lesson you learned, an idea that finally "clicked," etc.)

- **Special People** (relatives, friends, heroes, historical characters, etc.)

- **Special Places** (home, vacation spot, etc.)

- **Special Possessions** (books, games, toys, weapons, etc.)

EPIPHANY CHART

HIGH POINT

LOW POINT

TURNING POINT

SPECIAL PEOPLE

SPECIAL PLACES

SPECIAL POSSESSIONS

LESSON TWO
HOW TO READ POETRY

POETRY
read,
   memorize,
and recite

The **TITLE**
often contains info that
must be understood in
order for the reader to
comprehend the poem.

SETTING
      is the time in
which the poem
    takes place.

THANKFULNESS IN POETRY

Avid poetry readers grow into good poets. Reading lots of great poetry will not be much fun unless you enjoy it; this brings up a very important point. Whenever you begin to study something for the first time, you have a choice to make. Are you going to like this subject and relish it, or will it be sour to your taste and drive you away? You will find in your study of poetry, as in other subjects, if you determine to set your affections upon it from the beginning, you will have a delightful time learning to read and write poetry along the way.

When it is time to study poetry during the course of your week, think of it as a time in which you get to learn poetry instead of a time when you have to. In order to do this, choose to be thankful for the chance to learn about poetry. Poetry will not always be easy, but thankfulness and perseverance as you study will bring you greater learning and enjoyment. In short, teach yourself to love poetry.

READING POETRY

In this lesson you will learn how to *read*, *memorize*, and *recite* poetry that interests you. The first thing you should do, when you attempt a poem, is to read the title. This might seem too obvious to point out, but consider for a moment the importance of the title.

Often, in poetry, the title contains information that must be understood in order for the reader to comprehend the poem. The title might contain the *setting* of the poem, the time in which the poem takes place, or the name of a person the poem describes. After reading the title, guessing what the poem is about helps you to understand the title more fully. Then, read the poem quietly to yourself. As you read it, try to figure out how the poem should sound.

Just like in prose, when you read poetry, you pay attention to the punctuation. You shouldn't stop at the end of a line. Poetry, like music, has a distinct rhythm or beat that you need to detect. Finally, read the poem aloud, this time paying very close attention to what the poem means.

Here are the steps again:

STEP ONE: Read the **title** and guess what the poem is about.
　　　　　　　➠ The title is the key that unlocks the meaning of the poem.
STEP TWO: Read the poem silently to yourself to detect the **rhythm**.
　　　　　　　➠ Where should the beats be?
STEP THREE: Read the poem out loud to determine the **meaning**.
　　　　　　　➠ Pay attention to the punctuation.

When considering the poem's meaning, it is helpful to think in terms of *poetic categories*. These categories are based on the main subject or theme of the poem. Ask yourself what the poem was about. Most poems will naturally fall into at least one of the categories listed below. Of course, some poems will be a combination of the categories. Many historical poems tell a story resulting in what is called an *historical narrative*. If the story is a funny one, it could be described as a humorous historical narrative. If you are able to detect the type(s) of poetry you are reading, it helps you to understand its meaning.

POETIC CATEGORIES

NARRATIVE POETRY	Poems that tell stories
NATURE POETRY	Poems about creation
LOVE POETRY	Poems that sing of friendship or romantic love
DESCRIPTIVE POETRY	Poems that explain or describe something
HISTORICAL POETRY	Poems about countries, peoples, wars, etc.
RELIGIOUS POETRY	Poems about God or man's relationship with Him
HUMOROUS POETRY	Poems to make you laugh

PRACTICE

Read the following poems using all three steps described on the facing page, and then label the poetic category.

POETIC CATEGORY:

THE OWL AND THE FOX

There was an old Fox
  That lived under the rocks
At the foot of the huge oak tree;
  And of all of the foxes
  That ever did live
There was none so bad as he.
  His step was soft,
  With his padded feet,
But his claws were sharp beneath;
  And sharp were his eyes,
  And sharp were his ears,
And sharp were his terrible teeth.

  And the dreariest place
  You ever did see,
Was this old Fox's den;
  It was strewn with the down
  Of the tender Chick,
And the quills of the mother hen,
  Where he dragged them in
  This dismal den
And piled their bones together,
  And killed them dead,
  And sucked their blood,
  And ate their flesh,
  And picked their bones,
And warmed his bed with the feathers...
      – Unknown

POETIC CATEGORY:

FRAGMENT

Flower in the crannied wall,
I pluck you out of the crannies,
I hold you here, root and all, in my hand,
Little flower – but if I could understand
What you are, root and all, and all in all,
I should know what God and man is.
      – Alfred Tennyson

POETIC CATEGORY:

AMERICA THE BEAUTIFUL

O beautiful for spacious skies,
  For amber waves of grain,
For purple mountain majesties
  Above the fruited plain!
America! America!
  God shed His grace on thee
And crown thy good with brotherhood
  From sea to shining sea!
      – Katherine Lee Bates

POETIC CATEGORY: _____

POETIC CATEGORY: _____

TRINITY SUNDAY

Lord, who hast form'd me out of the mud,
  And hast redeem'd me through thy blood,
  And sanctifi'd me to do good;

Purge all my sins done heretofore:
  For I confess my heavy sore,
  And I will strive to sin no more.

Enrich my heart, mouth, hands in me,
  With faith, with hope, with charity;
  That I may run, rise, rest with thee.
         -George Herbert

SONNET XVIII

Shall I compare thee to a Summer's day?
Thou art more lovely and more temperate:
Rough winds do shake the darling buds of May,
And Summer's lease hath all too short a date:
Sometime too hot the eye of heaven shines,
And often is his gold complexion dimm'd;
And every fair from fair sometime declines,
By chance or nature's changing course untrimm'd:
But thy eternal Summer shall not fade
Nor lose possession of that fair thou ow'st;
Nor shall Death brag thou wander'st in his shade,
When in eternal lines to time thou grow'st:
  So long as men can breathe, or eyes can see,
  So long lives this, and this gives life to thee.
       – William Shakespeare

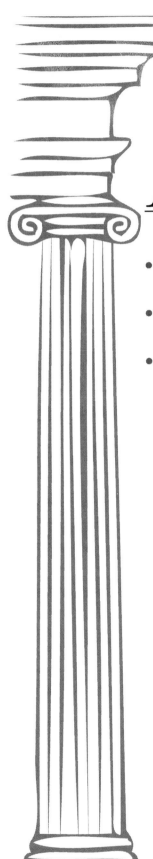

MODULE I

- SIMILE

- RHYME

- USING A RHYMING DICTIONARY

LESSON 3

SIMILE

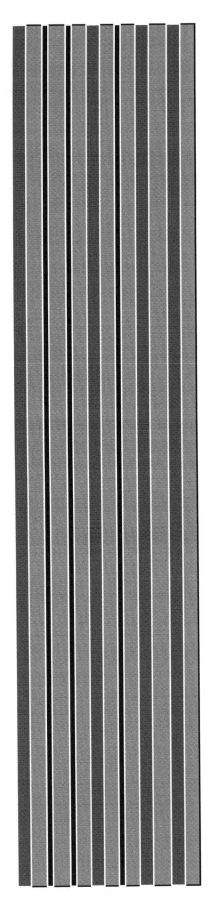

TROPE is a specific figure of speech.

1. SIMILE Compares two dissimilar things using the words **like, as,** or **than.**

When a poet compares two dissimilar things using the words *like*, as, or *than*, we call this trope a **simile**. A simile is a way of speaking that is not literal—not exactly true.

The words *like*, *as*, or *than* make these types of comparisons are explicit comparisons because it's obvious these two things are being compared.

Remember, to form a simile you must compare two *un-alike* things.

If I were to say,

"That hog eats like an animal,"

I would *not* have formed a simile because a hog is an animal.

Whereas, if I said,

"That man eats like a hog,"

the two things being compared are different enough to produce an effective picture in our minds.

An effective simile often produces a mental picture of the two compared objects.

PRACTICE

Circle the two dissimilar things being compared and underline like, as, or than in the following similes.

> ### EXAMPLE
> The poorly-mannered (schoolboy) ate <u>like</u> a (pig)

1. Her hair drooped round her pallid cheek, like seaweed on a clam.

2. On the abandoned and lifeless rocky island, a single lighthouse guarded the coastline

   like a loyal, solitary sentry.

3. The staff of his spear was like a weaver's beam.

4. She had cheeks like roses.

5. A fatal habit settles upon one like a vampire and sucks his blood.

6. A merry heart doeth good like a medicine, but a broken spirit drieth the bones. (Prov. 17:22)

7. The wrath of a king is as messengers of death: but a wise man will pacify it. (Prov. 16:14)

ACTIVITY 1

Write three of your own similes:

> ### EXAMPLE
> 1. My bike is as precious as a treasure chest.
>
> 2. Jackson, my friend, is as fast as a race car.
>
> 3. I am as thin as a pole.

1. _____

2. _____

3. _____

ACTIVITY 2

This is a poem of similes. We will discuss rhyming patterns in Lesson Four; however, it will help you to fill in the blanks if you first identify the words ending in exact sounding vowels and consonants. Fill in each blank so that the rhyming pattern is not broken.

1. As wet as a fish—as dry as a _____ ;   B
2. As live as a bird—as dead as a stone;   B
3. As plump as a partridge—as poor as a rat   A
4. As strong as a horse—as weak as a cat;   A
5. As hard as a flint—as soft as a mole;   _____
6. As white as a _____ —as black as coal;   _____
7. As plain as a staff—as rough as a bear;   _____
8. As light as a drum—as free as the ____ ;   _____
9. As heavy as lead—as light as a feather;   _____
10. As steady as time—uncertain as weather;   _____
11. As hot as an oven—as cold as a frog;   _____
12. As gay as a lark—as sick as a _____ ;   _____
13. As savage as tigers—as mild as a dove;   _____
14. As stiff as a poker—as limp as a glove;   _____
15. As blind as a bat—as deaf as a _____ ;   _____
16. As cool as a cucumber—as warm as toast;   _____
17. As flat as a flounder—as round as a ball;   _____
18. As blunt as a hammer—as sharp as an awl;   _____
19. As brittle as glass—as tough as gristle;   _____
20. As neat as a pin—as clean as a _____ ;   _____
21. As red as a rose—as square as a box;   _____
22. As bold as a thief—as sly as a _____ .   _____

ACTIVITY 3

Label each one of the following sentences as *simile* **or** *other*.

1. The rain looks like pearls upon a string. _____

2. My love is like a red, red rose. _____

3. That lion eats like an animal. _____

4. Mother smiled as she walked in the room. _____

5. The lips of the adulteress drip honey. _____

6. Her speech is as smooth as oil. _____

7. Your father's commandment is a lamp. _____

8. Your words are sharp as a two-edged sword. _____

9. He looks like he is hungry. _____

10. Children are like poppies spread about. _____

REVIEW

Define the following words in complete sentences.

1. poetry _____
   _____

2. trope _____
   _____

3. epiphany _____
   _____

4. simile _____
   _____

RIDDLE RENDEZVOUS

From time to time there will be one or two riddles at the bottom of your poetry worksheet. Some are posers and others are chestnuts, but all are just for fun and should be attempted after your work is completed! Can't figure it out? The answers are in the Teacher's Edition.

RIDDLE NO. 1

Runs over fields and woods all day
Under the bed at night sits not alone,
With long tongue hanging out,
A-waiting for a bone.

RIDDLE NO. 2

The beginning of eternity
The end of time and space
The beginning of every end,
And the end of every place.

LESSON 4

RHYME

A RHYME SCHEME is a combination of letters which represent the rhyming pattern of a poem. These letters are called **variables**.

STANZA is a paragraph of poetry.

BLANK VERSE is poetry that doesn't **rhyme**.

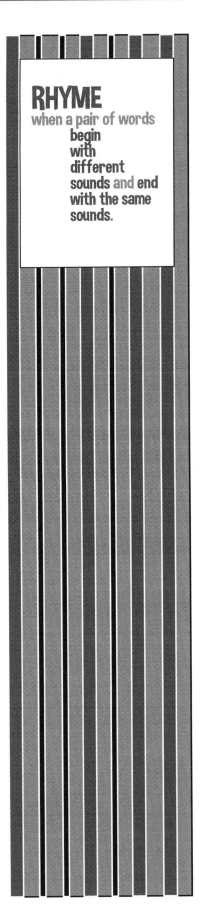

RHYME when a pair of words **begin** with **different sounds** and end **with the same sounds**.

When a pair of words begin with different sounds and end with the same sounds, we call it rhyme. Poetry doesn't have to rhyme; in fact, some of the best poetry (known as blank verse) does not rhyme. Rhyme, however, does help to cement lines together, to add beauty and additional layers of meaning to a poem.

The two different types of rhyme that we will initially concern ourselves with are full rhyme and slant rhyme. Skillful poets use full and slant rhyme to communicate the feelings they want the words to convey.

FULL RHYME: a pair of words ending with exact-sounding vowels and consonants (e.g. spring-wing, cat-hat). Full rhyme produces a clean and predictable effect.

SLANT RHYME: a pair of words ending with approximate-sounding vowels or consonants (e.g. death-earth, lectures-directors). Slant rhyme creates a feeling of tension or unease.

RHYME SCHEME

A rhyming poem's stanzas (paragraphs) follow a certain scheme. A rhyme scheme is a combination of letters which represent the rhyming pattern of a poem. These letters are called variables.

In order to determine the rhyme scheme of a poem, listen to the sound of the last word of the line. Label this line with an A. Read the next line. Does the last word of that line end with the same sound as the previous line? If it does, label it A. If it doesn't, label it with a B. Progress through the poem line by line labeling the matching end sounds with matching letters.

PRACTICE

Determine the rhyme schemes of the following stanzas. Label the last word of each line with a letter on the corresponding line. Lines whose last words share the same sound also share the same letter. In addition, write the rhyme scheme on the corresponding line.

EXAMPLE
RHYME SCHEME: A B A B C C C

Sweetest Saviour, if my soul

Were but worth the having,

Quickly should I then control

Any thought of waiving.

But when all my care and pains

Cannot give the name of gains

To thy wretch so full of stains,

What delight or hope remains?

RHYME SCHEME: ....

COUPLET: A STANZA WITH TWO LINES

Who read a chapter when they rise,

Shall ne're be troubled with ill eyes.

RHYME SCHEME: ....

TRIPLET: A STANZA WITH THREE LINES

Winds still work: it is their plot,

Be the season cold, or hot:

Hast thou sighs, or hast thou not?

RHYME SCHEME: _____

QUATRAIN: A STANZA WITH FOUR LINES

As Robin Hood in the forest strayed,   _____
All under the greenwood tree,   _____
He was aware of a brave young man,   _____
As fine as fine might be.   _____

But that thou art my wisdom, Lord,   _____
And both mine eyes are thine,   _____
My mind would be extremely stirr'd   _____
For missing my design.   _____

ACTIVITY

Choose three topics from your epiphany graph and write a simile about each one.

EXAMPLE
My father is as strong as a bear.

1. _____

2. _____

3. _____

REVIEW

Define the following words in complete sentences.

1. simile: _____
   _____

2. rhyme: _____
   _____

3. full rhyme: _____
   _____

4. slant rhyme: _____
   _____

5. stanza: _____
   _____

RIDDLE RENDEZVOUS

RIDDLE NO. 3

Without a bridle or a saddle,
Across a ridge I ride and straddle;
And every one, by help of me,

Though almost blind, is made to see
Then tell me pretty dame,
And witty master, what's my name?

LESSON 5
USING A RHYMING DICTIONARY

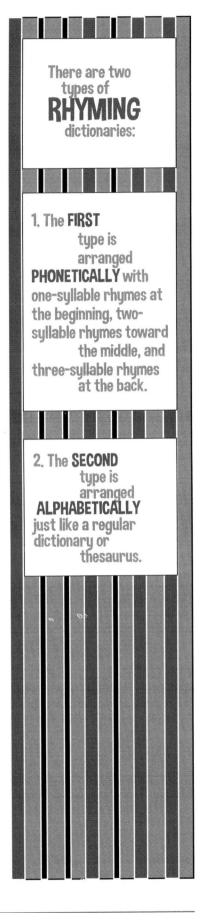

1. The **FIRST** type is arranged **PHONETICALLY** with one-syllable rhymes at the beginning, two-syllable rhymes toward the middle, and three-syllable rhymes at the back.

2. The **SECOND** type is arranged **ALPHABETICALLY** just like a regular dictionary or thesaurus.

As a budding poet, you should familiarize yourself with a rhyming dictionary. A good rhyming dictionary will aid in providing that difficult rhyme that has you stumped, and it will help to develop your vocabulary as you write.

In this lesson you will have an opportunity to better understand your rhyming dictionary and to practice using it. Take a look at your rhyming dictionary. There are two different types of rhyming dictionaries available.

The first type of rhyming dictionary is arranged phonetically with one syllable rhymes at the beginning, two syllable rhymes toward the middle, and three syllable rhymes at the back. An example of this type of dictionary is *The Complete Rhyming Dictionary*, by Clement Wood. In order to use this dictionary you must search for the phonetic sound that you are trying to match. Let's pretend that we want to rhyme the word *goat*:

STEP ONE: We must look in the monosyllable section under the sound /ōt/. You'll notice that the beginning of the monosyllable section starts with rhymes with the /a/ sound. Turn past /a/, /e/, and /i/ to get to /o/.

STEP TWO: Locate /ōt/ under which you should see entries such as *afloat, anecdote, antidote,* etc. These words may be used to rhyme with goat.

Now let's see if we can find two syllable words to rhyme with *waiting*. Remember the dictionary is arranged phonetically so you will need to look for the sound */ating/* which will come after the end of the monosyllable section of */u/* rhymes. If you are not sure about the phonetic spelling of a sound, check the front of your dictionary; it will have a phonetic key for vowels and consonants.

The second type of rhyming dictionary available is arranged alphabetically just like a regular dictionary or thesaurus (for example, *The Penguin Rhyming Dictionary*, by Rosalind Ferguson.) This rhyming dictionary will have two sections: the index where you look up the word you want to rhyme and the front section of rhyming groups.

With this dictionary, you simply look up the word in the index in the back and note the number listed after it. Then, you use the index number to locate the rhyming group in the front, and you will have a list of potential rhymes! The advantage to this type of dictionary is that you do not need to concern yourself with phonetic spellings at all.

Let's give it a try. Pretend that you are trying to find a rhyme for the word goat.	
STEP ONE:	Look up the word <u>goat</u> in the index.
STEP TWO:	Make note of the number written after the word goat. (_____)
STEP THREE:	Turn to the front of the book and find the rhyme section with the same number. You should find words such as oat, boat, coat, dote, bloat, gloat, etc. That's all there is to it!

PRACTICE

Use your rhyming dictionary to find five words that rhyme with each of the words and write them in the chart on the next page. Also, list the page number where the word was found in your rhyming dictionary. Four of the words must form a full rhyme and one must form a slant rhyme. Circle each slant rhyme.

EXAMPLE						
	PAGE NBR	(a)	(b)	(c)	(d)	(e)
1. pot	373	dot	cot	shot	lot	sit

EXAMPLE						
	PAGE NBR	(a)	(b)	(c)	(d)	(e)
2. cat	69	at	bat	scat	chat	flack

	PAGE NBR	(a)	(b)	(c)	(d)	(e)
1.	pot					
2.	cat					
3.	ship					
4.	lad					
5.	chief					
6.	green					
7.	haste					
8.	air					
9.	long					
10.	way					

ACTIVITY

1. Choose one word from the exercise above and write a poem using its rhyming words. This poem may be pure fiction and fantasy, but it should be understandable.

EXAMPLE

There once was a pot

He was sitting on a dot

In the middle of a cot,

Until finally he was shot.

_____

_____

_____

_____

2. Now select a different word and try the same activity again.

_____

_____

_____

_____

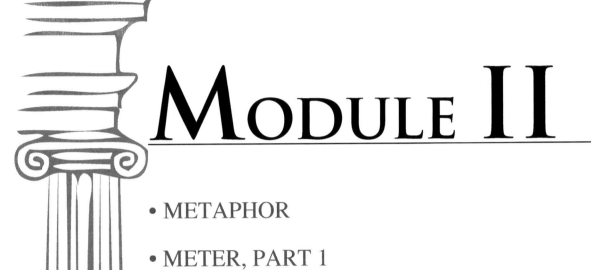

MODULE II

- METAPHOR

- METER, PART 1

- METER, PART 2

LESSON 6

METAPHOR

TROPE
is a specific
figure of speech.

1. SIMILE
Compares two dissimilar
things using the
words **like, as,** or
than. .

2. METAPHOR
is a figure of speech
in which an object
is being
CALLED
something
which **IT IS NOT**
because of a
SIMILARITY
between the two.

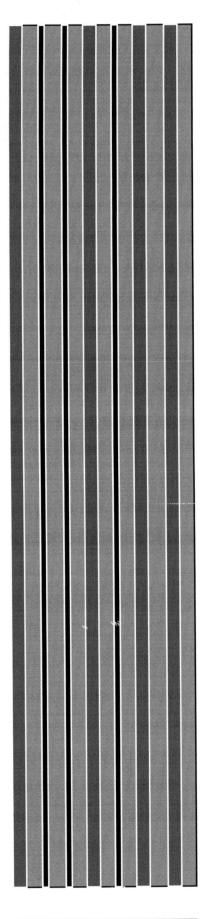

The second trope we will discuss is the metaphor. A **metaphor** is a figure of speech in which an object is being called something it is not because of a similarity between the two. When we compare two dissimilar objects without using the prepositions like, as, or than, we have created a **metaphor**. This trope expresses an implicit (not obvious) comparison.

As you consider the examples in the practice section, pay attention to how the objects being compared are not alike.

PRACTICE

Underline the objects being implicitly compared in the following metaphors.

EXAMPLE
When it comes to business, <u>Alfred</u> is a <u>fox</u>.

1. Life is a bowl of cherries.
2. The pianist's fingers, a raging storm, swirled over the keys.
3. All the world's a stage, and all the men and women merely players.
4. For the LORD God is a sun and shield. (Psalm 84:11)
5. Ye are the salt of the earth. (Matthew 5:13)
6. Take, eat; this is my body. . . this is my blood. (Matthew 26:26-28
7. I am the bread of life. (John 6:35)
8. I am the light of the world. (John 8:12)
9. I am the door: by me if any man enters in, he shall be saved. (John 10:9)
10. I am the vine, ye are the branches. (John 15:5)

ACTIVITY 1

Write three of your own metaphors.

EXAMPLE
The used car salesman was a <u>snake</u>.

1. _____

2. _____

3. _____

ACTIVITY 2

Rewrite the following metaphors as similes.

1. The fog was a heavy, wet blanket smothering the city.

    _____

2. Morning is a new sheet of paper for us to write on.

    _____

3. Spare moments are the gold-dust of time.

    _____

4. The night is a menacing stranger.

    _____

5. All the world's a stage.

    _____

REVIEW

Define the following words in complete sentences.

1. simile: _____

    _____

2. full rhyme: _____

    _____

3. slant rhyme: _____

    _____

4. metaphor: _____

    _____

RIDDLE RENDEZVOUS

RIDDLE NO. 4
What occurs once in a minute, twice in a moment, but never in an hour?

RIDDLE NO. 5
Give it food and it will live; give it water and it will die.

LESSON 7

METER, PART 1

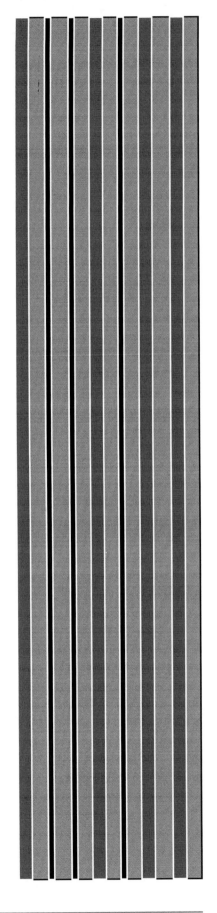

METER comes from the Greek word **METRON** (which means measure) and is defined as the measured rhythm of a line of poetry.

SYLLABLE is the smallest metrical unit of a line of poetry.

ACCENTED (/) = stress

UNACCENTED (◡) = breve

Meter comes from the Greek word *metron* (measure) and is defined as the measured rhythm of a line of poetry. The smallest metrical unit of a line of poetry is a syllable. The syllables in each line of poetry can be counted to determine the meter.

Each spoken-syllable in a line is either accented, designated by the symbol (/) called a stress, or unaccented, designated by the symbol (◡) called a breve [breev, brev].

SCANSION—In order to determine the meter of a poem, you must scan it. Initially we will cover the first two steps involved in scanning a poem using nursery rhymes because of the pronounced meter of these little ditties.

STEP ONE: Read the lines of the poem a number of times until you can feel or sense the rhythm.

STEP TWO: Mark the accented syllables of each line with the stress symbol (/) .

PRACTICE

Scan the following nursery rhymes, then mark the accented syllables of each line with the stress (/) symbol.

EXAMPLE
HICKORY DICKORY DOCK
/   /   /
Hickory, dickory, dock,
/   /   /
The mouse ran up the clock
/   /
The clock struck one,
/   /
The mouse ran down!
/   /   /
Hickory, dickory, dock.

DICKERY DICKERY DARE

Dickery, dickery, dare,

The pig flew up in the air.

The man in brown

Soon brought him down!

Dickery, dickery, dare.

THREE BLIND MICE

Three blind mice,

See how they run!

They all ran after a farmer's wife,

Who cut off their tails with a carving knife.

Did you ever see such a sight in your life,

As three blind mice?

MARY'S LAMB

Mary had a little lamb,

little lamb.

little lamb.

Mary had a little lamb,

Its fleece was white as snow.

As three blind mice?

JACK AND JILL

Jack and Jill went up the hill

To fetch a pail of water.

Jack fell down

And broke his crown

And Jill came tumbling after.

GEORGIE PORGIE

Georgie Porgie, puddin' and pie,

Kissed the girls and made them cry.

When the boys came out to play,

Georgie Porgie ran away.

THE FARMER IN THE DELL

The farmer in the dell,

The farmer in the dell,

Hi-ho, the derry-o,

The farmer in the dell.

PAT-A-CAKE

Pat-a-cake, pat-a-cake, baker's man,

Bake me a cake as fast as you can.

Roll it, and prick it, and mark it with a "B,"

And put it in the oven for Baby and me!

LITTLE MISS MUFFET

Little Miss Muffet

Sat on a tuffet

Eating her curds and whey;

Along came a spider;

Who sat down besider her

And frightened Miss Muffet away.

RIDDLE RENDEZVOUS

RIDDLE NO. 6

Thirty white horses on a red hill,

First they champ,

Then they stamp.

Then they stand still.

LESSON 8

METER, PART 2

METER comes from the Greek word **METRON** (which means measure) and is defined as the measured rhythm of a line of poetry.

SYLLABLE is the smallest metrical unit of a line of poetry.

ACCENTED
(/) = stress

UNACCENTED
(‿) = breve

Remember from our last lesson that meter is the measured rhythm of a line of poetry. The smallest piece of a line of poetry is a syllable. Each syllable that is heard in a line is either accented, designated by the symbol (/) called a *stress*, or unaccented, designated by the symbol (‿) called a *breve*.

It will also be helpful to remember that a word has as many syllables as it does vowel sounds. You may not count the vowels in order to determine the number of syllables, but you may count the vowel sounds which are heard when the word is pronounced.

Thus the word *speed* consists of one syllable because you can only hear one vowel sound, while the word *poet* consists of two syllables because you can hear two distinct vowel sounds. Take your time and learn to hear the meter in poetry before you begin labeling stresses and breves.

When the time comes for you to recite a poem, keep in mind that you do not read poetry the same way that you scan it. If you are not scanning, read and recite poetry naturally, paying attention to punctuation like you would in prose.

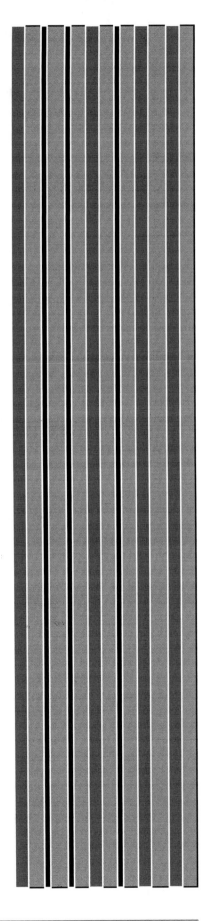

SCANSION

Now it is time to add the next step in scanning a poem. In this step you will mark the unaccented syllables. Each unaccented syllable in a line of poetry is labeled with a breve (◡).

The order that we will follow in this lesson—labeling the stressed syllables first and then the unstressed syllables—is very important to remember. You will have a very pleasant time scanning poetry if you remember…STRESSES FIRST!

STEP ONE: Read the lines of the poem a number of times until you can feel or sense the rhythm.

STEP TWO: Mark the accented syllables of each line with the stress symbol (/).

STEP THREE: Mark the unaccented syllables with the breve symbol (◡).

PRACTICE

Scan the following nursery rhymes.

EXAMPLE
HICKORY DICKORY DOCK
/ ◡ ◡ / ◡ ◡ /
Hickory, dickory, dock,
◡   /   ◡   /   ◡   /
The mouse ran up the clock
◡   /   ◡   /
The clock struck one,
◡   /   ◡   /
The mouse ran down!
/ ◡ ◡ / ◡ ◡ /
Hickory, dickory, dock.

DICKERY DICKERY DARE

Dickery, dickery, dare,

The pig flew up in the air.

The man in brown

Soon brought him down!

Dickery, dickery, dare.

JACK AND JILL

Jack and Jill went up the hill

To fetch a pail of water.

Jack fell down

And broke his crown

And Jill came tumbling after.

GEORGIE PORGIE

Georgie Porgie, puddin' and pie,

Kissed the girls and made them cry.

When the boys came out to play,

Georgie Porgie ran away.

THREE BLIND MICE

Three blind mice,

She how they run!

They all ran after a farmer's wife,

Who cut off their tails with a carving knife.

Did you ever see such a sight in your life,

As three blind mice?

THE FARMER IN THE DELL

The farmer in the dell,

The farmer in the dell,

Hi-ho, the derry-o,

The farmer in the dell.

PAT-A-CAKE

Pat-a-cake, pat-a-cake, baker's man,

Bake me a cake as fast as you can.

Roll it, and prick it, and mark it with a "B,"

And put it in the oven for Baby and me!

LITTLE MISS MUFFET

Little Miss Muffet

Sat on a tuffet

Eating her curds and whey;

Along came a spider;

Who sat down besider her

And frightened Miss Muffet away.

MARY'S LAMB

Mary had a little lamb,

little lamb.

little lamb.

Mary had a little lamb,

Its fleece was white as snow.

As three blind mice?

RIDDLE RENDEZVOUS

RIDDLE NO. 7
Remove the outside, cook the inside, eat the outside, throw away the inside.

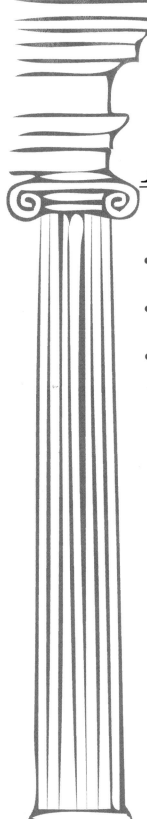

MODULE III

- PUN

- IAMB

- IAMBIC IMITATION

LESSON 9

PUN

> **TROPE** is a specific figure of speech.

> 1. SIMILE
> 2. METAPHOR

> **3. PUN** is a humorous use of words that sound **alike** or **nearly alike** but have different meanings.

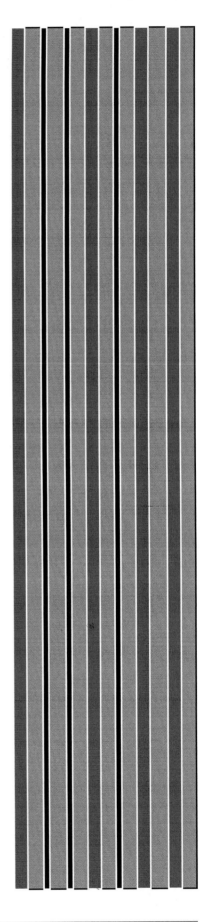

The third trope that we will study is the pun. A **pun** is a humorous use of words that sound alike or nearly alike but have different meanings. A pun may also be called a *play on words*.

Some critics have called the pun the lowest form of wit; however, many of the world's greatest writers have used puns very effectively.

Archie Armstrong was a Scottish jester employed at the court of Charles I. One day, in the presence of William Laud, the Archbishop of Canterbury, the jester asked to say grace. When his request was granted, Archie began:

> "Great praise be to God, and little Laud to the devil..."

The pun on his name infuriated the archbishop, who complained to the king, who then fired and banished the jester.

PRACTICE

Underline the word that is being played upon.

EXAMPLE

"Ask for me tomorrow and you shall find me a <u>grave</u> man. "

(From *Romeo and Juliet*, by William Shakespeare; Mercutio is speaking right after he was stabbed.)

---

1. Two silkworms were in a race. They ended up in a tie.
2. Eve was nigh Adam; Adam was naive.
3. Lance: "Did you hear that all of the members of King Arthur's Round Table have insomnia?"
   Merlin: "Wow! That's what I call having a lot of sleepless knights."
4. Atlas: "Hercules, what's a Greek urn?"
   Hercules: "Oh, about 40 drachmas a week."
5. "Tough luck!" said the egg in the monastery. "Out of the frying pan into the friar."
6. Always remember – no matter how bad prose may be, it might be verse.
7. Math teachers have lots of problems.
8. A neutron goes into a bar and asks the bartender, "How much for a drink?"
   The bartender replies, "For you, no charge."

ACTIVITY 1

See if you can track down three of your own puns this week.

1. _____
2. _____
3. _____

ACTIVITY 2

Scan the following nursery rhymes, making sure to follow the pattern below.

STEP ONE: Read the lines of the poem a number of times until you can feel or sense the rhythm.

STEP TWO: Mark the accented syllables of each line with the stress symbol (/) .

STEP THREE: Mark the unaccented syllables with the breve symbol (⌣).

EXAMPLE
JACK SPRAT

/   /   ⌣   /   ⌣   /

Jack Sprat could eat no fat,

⌣   /   ⌣   /   ⌣   /

His wife could eat no lean,

⌣   /   ⌣   /   ⌣   /   ⌣   /

And so betwixt the two of them

⌣   /   ⌣   /   ⌣   /

They licked the platter clean.

LITTLE JACK HORNER

Little Jack Horner

Sat in a corner,

Eating his mincemeat pie.

He stuck in his thumb

And pulled out a plum,

And said, "What a good boy am I!"

OLD KING COLE

Old King Cole was a merry old soul,

And a merry old soul was he.

He called for his pipe,

And he called for his bowl,

And he called for his fiddlers three.

PETER

Peter, Peter, pumpkin eater,

Had a wife and couldn't keep her.

He put her in a pumpkin shell

And there he kept her, very well.

HARK! HARK!

Hark! Hark! The dogs do bark,

The beggars are coming to town.

Some in rags,

And some in tags,

And one in a velvet gown!

QUEEN OF HEARTS

The Queen of Hearts

She made some tarts

All on a summer's day.

The Knave of Hearts,

He stole the tarts

And took them clean away.

REVIEW

Define the following words in complete sentences.

1. full rhyme

2. slant rhyme

3. meter

_____

_____

4. breve

_____

_____

RIDDLE RENDEZVOUS

RIDDLE NO. 8
The man who invented it, doesn't want it. The man who bought it, doesn't need it. The man who needs it, doesn't know it.

RIDDLE NO. 9
They come at night without being called and are lost in the day without being stolen.

LESSON 10

IAMB

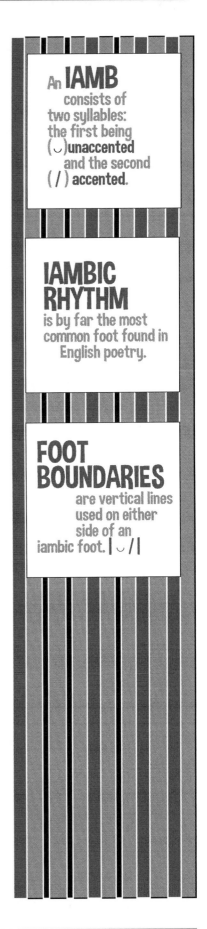

An **IAMB** consists of two syllables: the first being (◡) **unaccented** and the second (/) **accented**.

IAMBIC RHYTHM is by far the most common foot found in English poetry.

FOOT BOUNDARIES are vertical lines used on either side of an iambic foot. | ◡ / |

Remember from our previous studies that each syllable that is heard in a line is either accented, designated by the symbol (/) called a *stress*, or unaccented, designated by the symbol (◡) called a *breve*. Combinations of these syllables are described as **feet**. We will learn about four different types of feet in this text: iambic, trochaic, anapestic, and dactylic.

Iambic rhythm is by far the most common foot found in English poetry. An **iamb** consists of two syllables, the first being unaccented and the second accented | ◡ / | . We use vertical lines on either side of an iambic foot as foot boundaries as shown in the previous sentence.

The following words are iambic:

EXAMPLE	
◡ /	◡ /
| afraid |	| oppose |
◡ /	◡ /
| correct |	| delight |

SCANSION

In order to determine the meter of a poem you must scan it. After scanning a poem, you should know:

1. What type of feet the poem is made of,

2. How many feet there are in each line, and

3. What the rhyme scheme is.

You will need to memorize the following steps at this time.

STEP ONE: Read the lines of the poem a number of times until you can feel or sense the rhythm.

STEP TWO: Mark the accented syllables of each line with the stress symbol (/).

STEP THREE: Mark the unaccented syllables with the breve symbol ($\cup$) and insert foot boundaries (||).

STEP FOUR: Identify the predominate[1] foot type and the number of feet per line, and you will have the meter.

STEP FIVE: Label the rhyme scheme of the first stanza with variables.

Here are the rules again, stated more concisely, as a chant:

1. Sense the rhythm.
2. Mark the stress.
3. Breves and feet.
4. Meter, meter, what's my meter?
5. Label rhyme scheme.

NUMBER OF FEET PER LINE

Now, let's consider the number of feet per line. You can think of it as the number of steps you take across a line of poetry. Here are some of the possibilities:

NUMBER OF FEET PER LINE	
Monometer	1 foot per line
Dimeter	2 feet per line
Trimeter	3 feet per line
Tetrameter	4 feet per line
Pentameter	5 feet per line
Hexameter	6 feet per line
Heptameter	7 feet per line
Octameter	8 feet per line

---

1. Scansion is an inexact science, depending on the pronunciation of certain words. Also, most poets vary their feet to avoid monotony. For these reasons it is important to scan more than one line of a poem in order to identify the meter. As a rule we will scan the first three lines of each poem to determine its meter.

PRACTICE

Scan the iambic stanzas on the following page.

<table>
<tr><td colspan="2" align="center">**EXAMPLE**</td></tr>
</table>

METER / RHYME SCHEME
Iambic Dimeter — AAABCCCB

A MIDSUMMER NIGHT'S DREAM
by William Shakespeare

˘ / ˘ /	
| The rag | ing rocks |	A
˘ / ˘ /	
| And shiv' | ring shock |	A
˘ / ˘ /	
| Shall break | the locks |	A
˘ / ˘ /	
| Of pri | son gates, |	B
˘ / ˘ /	
| And Phi | bus' car |	C
˘ / ˘ /	
| Shall shine | from far, |	C
˘ / ˘ /	
|And make | and mar |	C
˘ / ˘ /	
|The fool | ish fates. |	B

METER / RHYME SCHEME

UPON HIS DEPARTURE HENCE
by Robert Herrick

Thus I

Pass by,

And die

As one

Unknown

and gone.

I'm made

A shade

And laid

I'th' grave;

There have

My cave,

Where tell

I dwell.

Farewell.

METER / RHYME SCHEME

EXCERPT FROM

VISION OF BELSHAZZAR
by Lord Byron

The monarch saw and shook,

And bade no more rejoice;

And bloodless waxed his look

And tremulous his voice.

METER / RHYME SCHEME

EXCERPT FROM

THE QUIP
by George Herbert

The merry world did on a day

With his train-bands and mates agree

To meet together, where I lay,

And all in sport to jeer at me.

ACTIVITY 1

Scan the following stanza and add three lines in iambic tetrameter.

METER / RHYME SCHEME

I lost my dog upon the shore

He would not follow to the shore,

I've called and called but no reply

RIDDLE RENDEZVOUS

RIDDLE NO. 10
Squeeze it and it cries tears as red as its flesh, but its heart is made of stone.

RIDDLE NO. 11
There is a certain crime, that if it is attempted, is punishable, but if it is committed, is not punishable. What is the crime?

LESSON 11

IAMBIC IMITATION

Scan the following iambic poem; then, with that meter in your ear, write your own poem using the same meter.

METER / RHYME SCHEME

_____

THE LAND OF STORY-BOOKS
by Robert Louis Stevenson

ˇ / ˇ / ˇ / ˇ /
At evening when the lamp is lit,

ˇ / ˇ / ˇ / ˇ /
Around the fire my parents sit;

ˇ / ˇ / ˇ / ˇ /
They sit at home and talk and sing,

ˇ / ˇ / ˇ / ˇ /
And do not play at anything.

Now, with my little gun I crawl

All in the dark along the wall,

And follow round the forest track

Away behind the sofa back.

So, when my nurse comes in for me,

Home I return across the sea,

And go to bed with backwards looks

At my dear land of Story-Books.

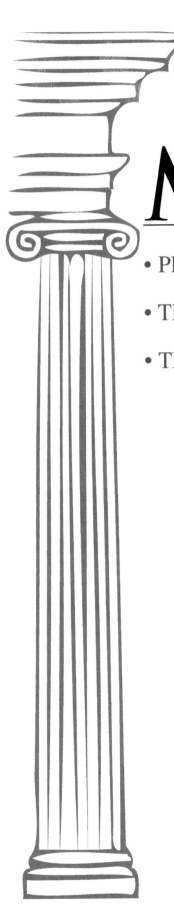

MODULE IV

- PERSONIFICATION

- TROCHEE

- TROCHAIC IMITATION

LESSON 12

PERSONIFICATION

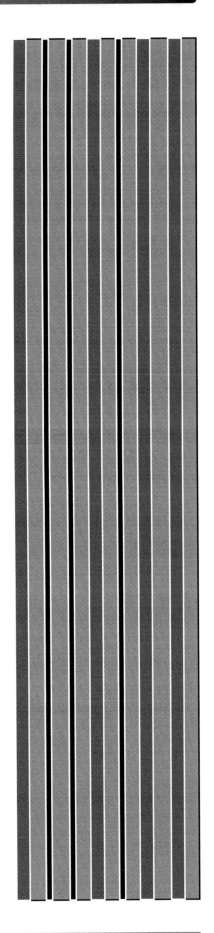

TROPE is a specific figure of speech.

1. SIMILE
2. METAPHOR
3. PUN

4.PERSONIFICATION
is a figure of speech in which a thing or idea is being represented as though it had **human** qualities or abilities.

Personification is a figure of speech in which a thing or idea is being represented as though it had human qualities or abilities (the qualities and abilities of a *person* – thus *person*ification).

PRACTICE

Underline the thing or idea that is being represented as a person.

EXAMPLE
The <u>heavens</u> declare the glory of God.

1. Sin lieth at the door... (Genesis 4:7)

2. The voice of thy brother's blood crieth unto me from the ground. (Genesis 4:10)

3. The land itself vomiteth out her inhabitants. (Leviticus 18:25)

4. Day unto day uttereth speech, and night unto night sheweth knowledge. (Psalm 19:2)

5. All my bones shall say, LORD, who is like unto thee... (Psalm 35:10)

6. Let the heavens rejoice, and let the earth be glad; let the sea roar, and the fullness thereof. Let the field be joyful, and all that is therein: then shall all the trees of the wood rejoice. (Psalm 98:11,12)

7. Then the moon shall be confounded, and the sun ashamed, when the Lord of hosts shall reign... (Isaiah 24:23)

8. Princes shall come out of Egypt; Ethiopia shall soon stretch out her hands unto God. (Psalm 68:31)

9. The surf clawed at the beach with its long, white fingers.

10. Confusion heard his voice.

ACTIVITY 1

Write three of your own examples of personification.

1. _____

2. _____

3. _____

ACTIVITY 2 - SCANSION REVIEW

Scan the following iambic poem by Alfred, Lord Tennyson and answer the questions below.

METER / RHYME SCHEME

_____

by Alfred, Lord Tennyson

He clasps the crag with crooken hands:

Close to the sun in lonely lands,

Ringed with the azure world, he stands.

The wrinkled sea beneath him crawls;

He watches from his mountain walls,

And like a thunderbolt he falls.

1. What would you title this poem? _____

2. Underline the tropes in the poem above—three personifications, one metaphor, and one simile.

ACTIVITY 3

Read through the essay below and underline all of the similes, metaphors, puns, and examples of personification you can find. Name each trope in the margin across from the line in which it was found.

SWINGING

by N. D. Wilson

The porch swing had always been old. It hung by the door and kept watch — 1
over the silent house. If it had ever been painted, it wasn't in this century. — 2
Chains rusted and wood like bone, the swing stole your trust and pleaded — 3
with you to sit and watch the fields ripple in the wind and the heat bake the — 4
grass. Here I sit and slowly rock, listening to the creaking of the swing describe — 5
to me the house, the fields, the well and the trees. The swing knows all the — 6
stories. And while I sit and listen, I become part of them. — 7

This is the house where my great granddad had been born a slave. From — 8
where I sit, I can see where he is now. This is the house where my grandma — 9
had been married, lived, bore my daddy, and died. This is the house, and this — 10
is the swing. — 11

I had come back to the house because I had to. I'd worked in Boston since — 12
high school. I had kept busy enough that at first I never noticed my ache. I — 13
had no family, I had never married, I had never vacationed, I had never lived. — 14
The guys at work had always invited me over for Thanksgiving and Christmas, — 15
and at first I had gone. Now I hadn't accepted the invitation in years. They'd — 16
done it because they pitied me. I'd gone because I'd pitied me. Now I was well — 17
beyond self pity. When I retired, they had thrown a party. They gave me beer, — 18
books, and had all chipped in and bought me a TV. I never watched it. — 19

For years after that I lived in a retirement village outside Boston. My pension — 20
was small but so was my place. I would pay my rent and buy my groceries and — 21
then I would stick the rest of my money in a box under the couch. At first — 22
the guys would still call me, but after awhile they forgot. I don't blame them. — 23
They had families. After dinner sometimes I would sit outside and listen to — 24
the noises from the other places. I could hear couples talking about health — 25
problems, pets and barbeques. I could listen, but I could never talk. Some — 26
times I would sit outside and play my guitar. I could make it talk to me, and I — 27
knew it was talking to my neighbors. They heard me play, and they knew that — 28
I was there. My guitar kept me from talking to myself. — 29

On my birthday, I would walk down the street to the little grocery store — 30
and buy a pint of ice cream. Then I would go home and listen to the noises of — 31
my neighbors and eat my celebration. I could never finish it. During the day I — 32
would work in my garden. (I had a garden. Sometimes I would play for it.) — 33

When I was younger, I had painted over my loneliness with hard work. I — 34
had tried to think that I was going somewhere and becoming someone. Now, — 35

I had no lies left to tell myself. I was nowhere. My life was over and I had gone _____ 36
no place. But what was worse was that I had gone no place with nobody. _____ 37
Nobody. My image of Heaven was a place where there was someone to talk _____ 38
to. Someone who would listen to me play my guitar. But I'd been to church _____ 39
before and I knew there was no such place. Now, more often than listening to _____ 40
my neighbors and pretending, I would listen and face the truth. My life was _____ 41
empty – no meaning, and no joy. I would sit in my door and look around the _____ 42
cul-de-sac at the lit windows, and I could hear the conversations that make _____ 43
up relationships. And I would cry, for I had neither of these things. I would cry _____ 44
until I was afraid my neighbors might hear, then I would go back into my place _____ 45
and cry for the shame of my wailing. _____ 46

I had lived this long. I had nothing better to do. Somebody said that despair _____ 47
like I had is deadly for a man, because it'll kill his want to live. That's not how _____ 48
it was with me. I was afraid of emptiness. So I woke up every morning scared, _____ 49
scared of the empty day ahead, and of the nothing it would bring. But that _____ 50
didn't mean I wanted to die. I knew the empty I would feel six feet under _____ 51
would make my life look exciting. _____ 52

The day before my eighty-sixth birthday I woke up knowing I was beat. _____ 53

I didn't want to die, but I knew death was all that was left for me. I got up, ate _____ 54
breakfast, and went outside and watered my plants. When I came back inside _____ 55
I knew I was going to run. I had to change something. A long life was behind _____ 56
me, but I was still too scared to die. What I wanted was to find somewhere _____ 57
that meant something. Something for me. I put clothes into a bag with all the _____ 58
money from under the couch. I needed to say goodbye to my place and my _____ 59
neighbors, so I took my guitar outside and played. I played longer than I had _____ 60
ever played before and a lady even came outside to listen. Then I slung my _____ 61
guitar over my shoulder and, carrying my bag, I headed off for the bus station. _____ 62

It had taken me a day and a half, but I had found the house. Still sitting _____ 63
back between the two hills, with the big elms in front. Still surrounded by hay _____ 64
fields. It was empty and dead to the rest of the world, but not to me. The last _____ 65
time I sat in that swing, I'd been fifteen. Come out of town to watch my great _____ 66
uncle get buried. The swing still remembered me. It remembered my daddy _____ 67
and my granddaddies. _____ 68

Now I sat in the swing. And I listened, just like I had listened to my neighbors, _____ 69
only they hadn't been talking to me. I listened to all the stories and watched _____ 70
the fields and the trees. I watched the hills, and they listened too. _____ 71

I heard about my great granddad, and how strong he'd been. How he'd _____ 72
been so strong that his master had him tug o' war with one of the mules. And _____ 73
how his master gave him five dollars when he won. I heard and I laughed, and _____ 74
the trees and the fields laughed, because they remembered. The swing told _____ 75
me about how he'd met my granny, and how the master had married them. _____ 76
It told about how he died fighting in the hay field across the creek. And I was _____ 77
proud that he was mine. _____ 78

I sat in the swing and laughed. The swing rocked and creaked, and told _____ 79
all it knew to its prodigal son. It forgave me for coming so late and so did the _____ 80
house and the fields. They forgave and embraced me. They told me where I _____ 81
was from, and what I was, and to them I was not empty. To them I was part of _____ 82
a picture. A picture of joy and even of sorrow. But not of emptiness. _____ 83

While I sat and laughed with the trees and fields, while I listened to the _____ 84
swing creak its story, I loved. I loved my granddad and his young bride. I loved _____ 85
my great granddad and his courage, I loved my grandma's cooking and my _____ 86
momma's dog. I loved my family and I loved where I came from. I learned _____ 87
what it was to sacrifice from my grandad and I wept at his death. I learned _____ 88
what joy was and the meaning of sorrow. I had no sorrow before. I had only _____ 89
emptiness. _____ 90

Then the swing told me about me. It told me about how I had tried to climb _____ 91
the big elm out front in my Sunday best after Great Uncle Toby's funeral, and _____ 92
about the whipping I got for it. It told me about how I'd fallen down the stairs _____ 93
in the back and lost two teeth. It brought back old and long dead memories _____ 94
of who I was. And then it told me about my momma's death and how my _____ 95
daddy had moved us to the city, so I could get learning. It told sad stories of _____ 96
moves and deaths, and then the quiet. _____ 97

When it finished its stories, my eyes were swimming but I wasn't crying. _____ 98
Then I told them my story. I got out my guitar and they listened. I looked out _____ 99
at the fields below while I sang. I watched the trees sway and the wind climb _____ 100
the hills. The swing rocked gently with my story. They listened to me, the same _____ 101
way they had watched my granddaddy and my momma. And my story wasn't _____ 102
a sad one. I had a strong daddy, and a strong great granddaddy. My momma _____ 103
loved me and my granny could make the best strawberry pie. They listened to _____ 104
my story, but my story had changed. It was full. Full of love and joy for a family _____ 105
I was part of. And when I'd finished my story, I just kept on swinging. _____ 106

Now I sit and watch the sun set over the hills where my granddaddy died, _____ 107
just another sunset in the swing's story, and I think about all the things that _____ 108
happened here at this house, in this swing, beneath those trees and on those _____ 109
hills. I think about all my family, and I laugh. I know that death isn't empty. _____ 110

RIDDLE RENDEZVOUS

RIDDLE NO. 12
What can run but never walks, has a mouth but never talks, has a head but never weeps, has a bed but never sleeps?

RIDDLE NO. 13
It is weightless, you can see it, and if you put it in a barrel, it will make the barrel lighter.

LESSON 13

TROCHEE

A TROCHEE consists of **two syllables:** the first being (/) **accented** and the second (◡) **unaccented.**

A TROCHAIC FOOT | / ◡ | is the mirror image of an Iamb. | ◡ / |.

A DANGLER is a lone breve or stress or even a combination of the two—labeled as a separate foot.

A trochaic foot, or *trochee* [troh-kee], consists of two syllables; the first being accented and the second unaccented | / ◡ |. Notice that a trochaic foot is the mirror image of an iamb | ◡ / |. The following words are trochaic: *gather, going, heartless, laughter*.

EXAMPLE	
/ ◡	/ ◡
gather	heartless
/ ◡	/ ◡
going	laughter

IRREGULARITIES

Many times a poet will vary his meter in order to make it more intricate or interesting. When you run into some irregularities as you scan poetry, don't panic. Follow the first three rules of scansion. Label the accented syllables first and then the unaccented ones; once this is done, take a careful look at each line.

Look for patterns (iambic, trochaic) that you can group with foot boundaries, and if you end up with a "dangler"—a lone breve or stress or even a combination of the two—label it as its own separate foot. Remember to look for the predominate meter when you scan. You will find danglers in the stanzas below; just smile and keep on scanning.

PRACTICE

Scan the following trochaic stanzas.

EXAMPLE

METER / RHYME SCHEME
Trochaic Tetrameter - ABAB

Excerpt From **AN ASSURANCE**
by Nicholas Breton

/ ᴜ / ᴜ / ᴜ
| Say that | I should | love thee, | A

/ ᴜ / ᴜ / ᴜ / ᴜ
| Would you | say 'tis | but a | saying? | B

/ ᴜ / ᴜ / ᴜ / ᴜ
| But if | love in | prayers | move ye, | A

/ ᴜ / ᴜ / ᴜ / ᴜ
| Will you | not be | moved with | praying? | B

METER / RHYME SCHEME

Excerpt From **A CRADLE HYMN**
by Isaac Watts

Soft and easy is thy cradle:

Coarse and hard thy Savior lay,

When His birthplace was a stable

And His softest bed was hay.

METER / RHYME SCHEME

Excerpt From **MACBETH**
by William Shakespeare

Round about the cauldron go;

In the poisoned entrails throw.

Toad, that under cold stone

Days and nights has thirty-one

Sweltered venom sleeping got,

Boil thou first i' the charmed pot.

METER / RHYME SCHEME

Excerpt From **THE REVENGE**
by Thomas Chatterton

Humming,

Thrumming,

Groaning,

Toning,

Squeeking

METER / RHYME SCHEME

Excerpt From **SOLDIER, REST! THY WARFARE O'ER**
by Sir Walter Scott

Soldier rest! thy warfare o'er,

Sleep the sleep that knows not breaking:

Dream of battled fields no more,

Days of danger, nights of waking.

In our isle's enchanted hall,

Hands unseen thy couch are strewing,

Fairy strains of music fall,

Every sense in slumber dewing.

Soldier, rest! thy warfare o'er,

Dream of fighting fields no more;

Sleep the sleep that knows not breaking,

Morn of toil, nor night of waking.

ACTIVITY 1

Scan the following stanza and add three lines in trochaic tetrameter.

METER / RHYME SCHEME

Sharks, they swam about my head

Spinning through an ocean bed,

From behind I felt a tug

ACTIVITY 2

Scan the following stanza and add three lines in iambic tetrameter.

METER / RHYME SCHEME

Alone and tired cried the lad,

Evr'y piece of food he'd had,

Was taken by that awful fox,

LESSON 14
TROCHAIC IMITATION
METER / RHYME SCHEME

HAPPY SONGS
by William Blake

Piping down the valleys wild,

Piping songs of pleasant glee,

On a cloud I saw a child,

And he, laughing, said to me,

"Pipe a song about a lamb,"

So I piped with merry cheer;

"Piper, pipe that song again,"

So I piped, he wept to hear.

"Drop thy pipe, thy happy pipe,

Sing thy songs of happy cheer."

So I sang the same again,

While he wept with joy to hear.

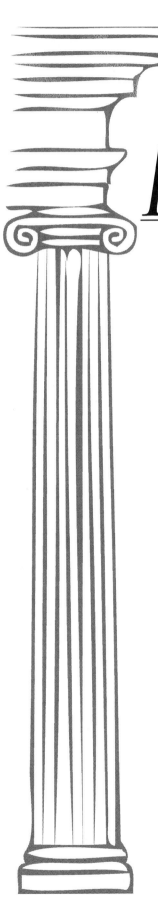

MODULE V

- SYNECDOCHE

- ANAPEST

- ANAPESTIC IMITATION

LESSON 15

SYNECDOCHE

TROPE is a specific figure of speech.

1. SIMILE
2. METAPHOR
3. PUN
4. PERSONIFICATION

5. SYNECDOCHE is a trope in which **some** striking part of an object stands for **the whole** or **the whole for the part.**

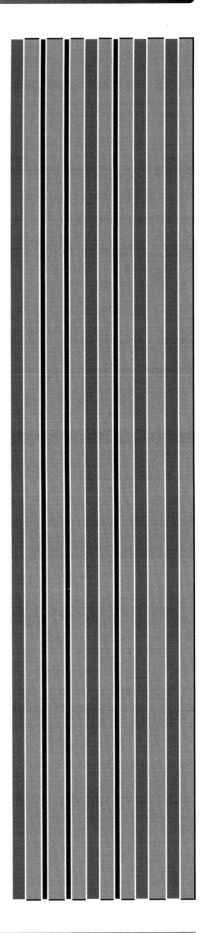

We have covered four figures of speech so far: simile, metaphor, pun, and personification. The fifth picture that we will learn about is called synecdoche. *Synecdoche* is a trope in which some striking part of an object stands for the whole or the whole for the part.

Let's consider the example, "All hands on deck!" Obviously, the ship's captain does not want his deck littered with disembodied hands. He wants all the sailors to bring their hands to work. The hands represent the whole.

PRACTICE

Underline the part and write the whole that it represents on the line.

EXAMPLE	
All <u>hands</u> on deck!	sailors

1. We have five hundred head of longhorns. _____

2. Look at my new set of wheels! _____

3. We await word from the crown. _____

4. And Abram took Sarai his wife. . . and the souls that they had gotten in Haran. (Genesis 12:5) _____

5. Absalom stole the hearts of the men of Israel. (2 Samuel 15:6) _____

6. O thou that hearest prayer, unto thee shall all flesh come. (Psalm 65:2) _____

7. For their feet run to evil. (Proverbs 1:16) _____

ACTIVITY 1

Write three of your own examples of synecdoche.

1. _____

2. _____

3. _____

ACTIVITY 2

Scan the following stanzas. Be careful to distinguish between iambic and trochaic meter.

METER / RHYME SCHEME

Excerpt From **ONE WORD MORE**
by Robert Browning

This of verse alone, one life allows me;

Verse and nothing else have I to give you.

METER / RHYME SCHEME

Excerpt From **THE CHRISTIAN STOIC**
by Thomas Campion

The man whose silent days

In harmless joys are spent,

Whom hopes cannot delude,

Nor sorrow discontent;

METER / RHYME SCHEME

Excerpt From **THE RAPE OF THE LOCK: CANTO 3**
by Alexander Pope

The hungry Judges soon the sentence sign,

And wretches hang that jurymen may dine.

METER / RHYME SCHEME

Excerpt From **THE DANCE OF THE DEATH**
by Sir Walter Scott

But still the corn

At dawn of morn

At eve lies waste,

A trampled paste.

REVIEW 1

Define the following words in complete sentences.

1. simile

2. full rhyme

3. personification

4. synecdoche

REVIEW 2

Identify the following figures of speech/tropes (simile, metaphor, pun, personification or synecdoche).

_____

_____

_____

_____

_____

_____

_____

_____

_____

1. There moved the multitude, a thousand heads.
2. Friendship is a sheltering tree.
3. The bride hath paced into the hall, Red as a rose is she.
4. The hot pink sweater grabbed her attention.
5. He is a stubborn ox.
6. Springtime bounded into hot Summer's lusty arms and expired.
7. The trees by the shores shone like copper and like blood.
8. They stood terrified with leaping shadows of dense black at their feet.
9. The kettle is boiling.
10. "I'm dying!" he croaked.

RIDDLE RENDEZVOUS

RIDDLE NO. 14
We are little creatures;   all of us have different features.   One of us in glass is set;   one of us you'll find in jet.   Another you may see in tin,   and the fourth is boxed within.   If the fifth you should pursue,   it can never fly from you.   What are we?

[This page intentionally left blank]

LESSON 16

ANAPEST

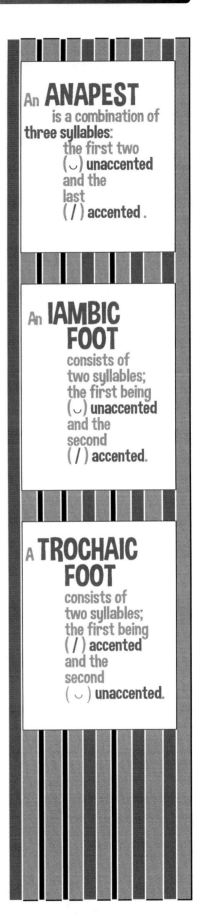

An **ANAPEST** is a combination of **three syllables:** the first two ($\cup$) **unaccented** and the last ($/$) **accented** .

An **IAMBIC FOOT** consists of two syllables; the first being ($\cup$) **unaccented** and the second ($/$) **accented.**

A **TROCHAIC FOOT** consists of two syllables; the first being ($/$) **accented** and the second ($\cup$) **unaccented.**

At this point we have covered two different foot types: iambic | $\cup$ / | and trochaic | / $\cup$ |.

The foot that we will learn about in this lesson is a combination of three syllables instead of two. An *anapest* is a combination of three syllables, the first two unaccented and the last accented | $\cup$ $\cup$ / |.

The following words are anapestic:

EXAMPLE	
$\cup$ $\cup$ /	$\cup$ $\cup$ /
appertain		Isabelle	
$\cup$ $\cup$ /	$\cup$ $\cup$ /
interrupt		disappear	

Remember to look for patterns and not to panic if you end up with a dangler. Look for some variation in foot type in the stanzas on the next page. Some of those anapestic stanzas have danglers and iambic feet in them. Persevere!

PRACTICE

Scan the following anapestic stanzas.

EXAMPLE
METER / RHYME SCHEME
Anapestic Tetrameter — AABB

Excerpt From THE DESTRUCTION OF SENNACHERIB

by Lord Byron

```
   ᵕ   ᵕ  /  ᵕ   ᵕ      /    ᵕ   ᵕ  /  ᵕ   ᵕ  /
```
| The Assyri | an came down | like the wolf | on the fold, | A

```
   ᵕ   ᵕ  /  ᵕ    ᵕ     /    ᵕ  ᵕ /  ᵕ   ᵕ  /
```
| And his co | horts were gleam | ing in pur | ple and gold; | A

```
   ᵕ   ᵕ     /    ᵕ   ᵕ     /   ᵕ   ᵕ    /  ᵕ   ᵕ  /
```
| And the sheen | of their spears | was like stars | on the sea, | B

```
   ᵕ    ᵕ   /    ᵕ    ᵕ    /  ᵕ  ᵕ  /  ᵕ  ᵕ /
```
| When the blue | wave rolls night | ly on deep | Galilee. | B

METER / RHYME SCHEME

_____

Excerpt From MANFRED

by Lord Byron

On the form of thy birth,   _____

Of the mould of thy clay,   _____

Which return'd to the earth,   _____

Reappear to the day!   _____

METER / RHYME SCHEME

Excerpt From **THE LADY OF THE LAKE: CANTO 3**
by Sir Walter Scott

He is gone on the mountain,

He is lost to the forest,

Like a summer-dried fountain,

When our need was the sorest,

The font, re-appearing,

From the raindrops shall borrow,

But to us come no cheering,

To Duncan no morrow!

METER / RHYME SCHEME

Excerpt From **ESCAPE AT BEDTIME**
by Robert Lewis Stevenson

The lights from the parlor and kitchen shone out

Through the blinds and the windows and bars

And high overhead and all moving about,

There were thousands of millions of stars.

There ne'er were such thousands of leaves on a tree,

Nor of people in church or the park,

As the crowds of the stars that looked down upon me,

And that glittered and winked in the dark.

ACTIVITY 1

Scan the following stanza and add three lines in anapestic tetrameter.

METER / RHYME SCHEME

The great giant he rumbled he tumbled from bed,

He was crying and sweating, he'd broken his head,

Then a look of surprise came across his huge face.

ACTIVITY 2

Scan the following stanza and add three lines in iambic pentameter / hexameter.

METER / RHYME SCHEME

Alone and shaking was the feathered hen,

Unknowing soon she would be taken from her pen.

Oh fatal day they led her through the yard,

ACTIVITY 3

Scan the following stanza and add three lines in trochaic pentameter.

METER / RHYME SCHEME

Skins of onions, rancid bits of meat,

Sickness prospered cleanliness has fled,

Skinny dogs now wander in the street,

RIDDLE RENDEZVOUS

RIDDLE NO. 15
Here on Earth it's always true, that a day follows a day. But there is a place where yesterday always follows today!

LESSON 17

ANAPESTIC IMITATION

Scan the following anapestic poem; then, with that meter in your ear, write your own poem using the same meter.

METER / RHYME SCHEME

THE DESTRUCTION OF SENNACHERIB
by George Gordon, Lord Byron

1st Stanza

The Assyrian came down like the wolf on the fold

And his cohorts were gleaming in purple and gold;

And the sheen of their spears was like stars on the sea,

When the blue wave rolls nightly on deep Galilee.

2nd Stanza

Like the leaves of the forest when summer is green,

That host with their banners at sunset were seen:

Like the leaves of the forest when autumn hath blown,

That host on the morrow laid withered and strown.

3rd Stanza

For the Angel of Death spread his wings on the blast,

And breathed in the face of the foe as he passed;

And the eyes of the sleepers waxed deadly and chill,

And their hearts but once heaved, and forever grew still!

In the blanks below, write your own poem using the same meter as Byron's.

MODULE VI

- HYPERBOLE

- DACTYL

- DACTYLIC IMITATION

LESSON 18

HYPERBOLE

TROPE is a specific figure of speech.

1. SIMILE
2. METAPHOR
3. PUN
4. PERSONIFICATION
5. SYNECDOCHE

6.HYPERBOLE is a figure of speech in which an **extravagant exaggeration** is made in order to add force or intensity to a statement. Hyperbole comes from the Greek word meaning **excess**.

A *hyperbole* is a figure of speech in which an *extravagant exaggeration* is made in order to add force or intensity to a statement. Hyperbole comes from a Greek word meaning *excess*.

EXAMPLE
There was a young lady of Lynn Who was so uncommonly thin That when she essayed To drink lemonade, She slipped through the straw and fell in.

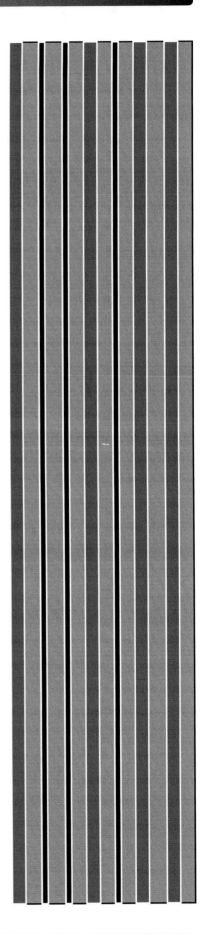

PRACTICE

Underline the word or phrase which is an exaggeration, and write a more literal word or phrase on the blank.

EXAMPLE	
The vase fell off the counter and broke into a <u>million</u> pieces.	three thousand, two hundred, fifty-six

1. My back is killing me.
2. I've told you a million times not to exaggerate.
3. Is it lunch time? I'm starving!
4. Dr. Johnson drank his tea in oceans.
5. I nearly died laughing!
6. She was hopping mad.
7. I tried a thousand times.
8. The cities are great and walled up to heaven. (Deut. 1:28)
9. Tropes are everywhere!
10. The Pharisees therefore said among themselves...behold, the world is gone after him. (Jn. 12:19)

ACTIVITY 1

Write three of your own examples of hyperbole.

_____

_____

_____

ACTIVITY 2

Scan the following stanzas. Be careful to distinguish between iambic, trochaic and anapestic meter
.

METER / RHYME SCHEME

Excerpt From **STANZAS TO AUGUSTA**
by Lord Byron

Though the rock of my last hope is shivered,

And its fragments are sunk in the wave,

METER / RHYME SCHEME

Excerpt From **MY MIND TO ME A KINGDOM IS**
by Sir Edward Dyer

My wealth is health and perfect ease;

My conscience clear my chief defense.

METER / RHYME SCHEME

Excerpt From **THE BLACKBIRD**
by Baron Alfred Tennyson

O blackbird! sing me something well:

While all the neighbors shoot the round,

I keep smooth plats of fruitful ground,

Where thou may'st warble, eat and dwell.

METER / RHYME SCHEME

Excerpt From **THE TIGER**
by William Blake

Tiger! Tiger! burning bright

In the forests of the night,

What immortal hand or eye

Could frame thy fearul symmetry?

REVIEW

Define the following words in complete sentences.

1. foot

2. rhyme

3. iamb

4. trochee

5. anapest

RIDDLE RENDEZVOUS

RIDDLE NO. 16

As I was going to St. Ives

I met a man with seven wives.

Each wife had seven sacks

Each sack had seven cats,

Each cat had seven kits.

Kits, cats, sacks, and wives,

How many were going to St. Ives?

LESSON 19

DACTYL

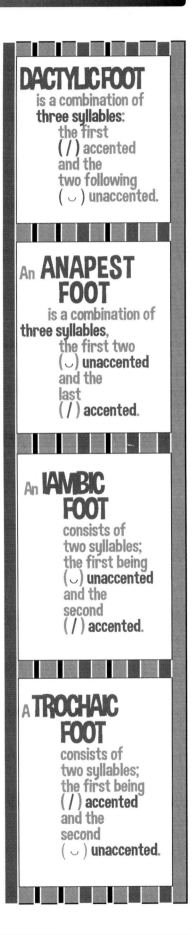

DACTYLIC FOOT
is a combination of
three syllables:
the first
(/) accented
and the
two following
(‿) unaccented.

An **ANAPEST FOOT**
is a combination of
three syllables,
the first two
(‿) **unaccented**
and the
last
(/) **accented.**

An **IAMBIC FOOT**
consists of
two syllables;
the first being
(‿) **unaccented**
and the
second
(/) **accented.**

A **TROCHAIC FOOT**
consists of
two syllables;
the first being
(/) **accented**
and the
second
(‿) **unaccented.**

Dactyl literally means *finger—that which has three joints.* As a finger has three sections, the first being the longest, so a dactylic foot has three syllables, the first being the longest.

A *dactylic foot* is a combination of three syllables, the first accented and the two following unaccented | / ‿ ‿ |. Notice that this is the mirror image of the anapest.

The following words are dactylic:

EXAMPLE	
/ ‿ ‿ | happiness |	/ ‿ ‿ | drearily |
/ ‿ ‿ | satisfy |	/ ‿ ‿ | merriment |
/ ‿ ‿ | century |	

PRACTICE

Scan the following dactylic stanzas.

EXAMPLE

METER / RHYME SCHEME

Dactylic Hexameter—Blank Verse

Excerpt From **EVANGELINE**

by Henry Wadsworth Longfellow

/ ∪ ∪　/ ∪ ∪　/ ∪ ∪　/ ∪ ∪　/ ∪ ∪　/ ∪

|This is the | forest pri | meval, The | murmuring | pines and the | hemlocks |

/ ∪ ∪　/ ∪ ∪　/ ∪ ∪　/ ∪ ∪　/ ∪ ∪　/ ∪

| Bearded with | moss, and in | garments of | green, indis | tinct in the | twilight. |

METER / RHYME SCHEME

Excerpt From **SONG OF CLAN-ALPINE**

by Sir Walter Scott

Hail to the chief who in triumph advances!

Honored and blest be the evergreen pine!

Long may the tree in his banner that glances,

Flourish, the shelter and grace of our line!

METER / RHYME SCHEME

_____

Excerpt From **THE CHARGE OF THE LIGHT BRIGADE**
by Baron Alfred Tennyson

Cannon to the right of them,

Cannon to the left of them,

Cannon in front of them

Volleyed and thundered;

Stormed at with shot and shell,

Boldly they fought, and well.

METER / RHYME SCHEME

_____

Excerpt From **RUGBY CHAPEL**
by Matthew Arnold

And there are some, whom a thirst

Ardent, unquenchable, fires,

Not with the crowd to be spent,

Not without aim to go round

In an eddy of purposeless dust,

Effort unmeaning and vain.

ACTIVITY 1

Scan the following stanza and add three lines in dactylic tetrameter.

METER / RHYME SCHEME

Falling from airplanes is always quite fright'ning

Losing your balance and falling head first

But if you think of it as though you're sailing

LESSON 20

DACTYLIC IMITATION

Scan the following dactylic poem; then, with that meter in your ear, write your own using the same meter.

METER / RHYME SCHEME

—

THE LABORATORY

by Robert Browning

1st Stanza

Grind away, moisten and mash up thy paste,

Pound at thy powder,—I am not in haste!

Better sit thus, an observe thy strange things,

Than go where men wait me and dance at the King's.

2nd Stanza

That in the mortar—you call it a gum?

Ah, the brave tree whence such gold oozings come!

And yonder soft phial, the exquisite blue,

Sure to taste sweetly,—is that poison too?

3rd Stanza

Had I but all of them, thee and thy treasures,

What a wild crowd of invisible pleasures!

To carry pure death in an earring, a casket,

A signet, a fan-mount, a filligree-basket!

In the blanks below, write your own poem using the same meter as Browning's.

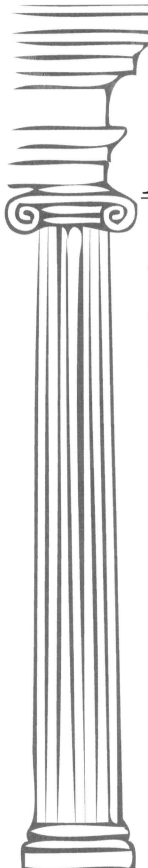

MODULE VII

- ONOMATOPOEIA

- ALLITERATION

- ALLITERATIVE IMITATION

LESSON 21

ONOMATOPOEIA

TROPE is a specific figure of speech.

1. SIMILE
2. METAPHOR
3. PUN
4. PERSONIFICATION
5. SYNECDOCHE
6. HYPERBOLE

7. ONOMATOPOEIA is a figure of speech in which words are used that **sound** like what they mean.

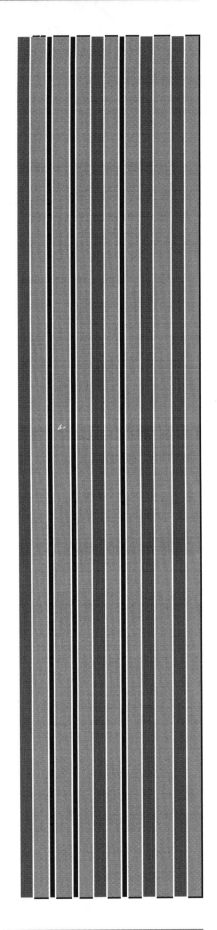

The seventh trope is called onomatopoeia. *Onomatopoeia* is a figure of speech in which words are used that *sound* like what they mean. Essentially, you're creating a word or naming a sound.

Hum, whiz, crash, twitter, whir, plop, peep, clink, meow, crackle, slush, swish, jangle, and crunch are all onomatopoetic words.

The following are onomatopoetic words:

EXAMPLE			
hum	whiz	crash	twitter
whir	plop	peep	clink
meow	crackle	slush	swish
jangle	crunch		

PRACTICE

Underline the word or words in the following stanzas that are onomatopoetic.

EXAMPLE

<u>Baa</u>, <u>baa</u>, black sheep,
Have you any wool?
Yes, sir, yes, sir,
Three bags full.
—Mother Goose

Excerpt From **THE RIME OF THE ANCIENT MARINER**
by Samuel Taylor Coleridge

The ice was here, the ice was there,
The ice was all around.
It cracked and growled, and roared and howled,
Like noises in a swound!

Excerpt From **THE BELLS**
by Edgar Allan Poe

Hear the sledges with the bells–
Silver bells!
What a world of merriment their melody foretells!
How they tinkle, tinkle, tinkle,
In the icy air of night!
While the stars that oversprinkle
All the heavens, seems to twinkle
With a crystalline delight;
Keeping time, time, time,
In a sort of Runic rhyme,
To the tintinnabulation that so musically wells
From the bells, bells, bells, bells,
Bells, bells, bells–
From the jingling and the tinkling of the bells.

ACTIVITY 1

Write your own examples of onomatopoetic words that represent the following sounds:

1. A soda-pop can being opened _____
2. Coins being tossed into a glass _____
3. An egg hitting the sidewalk _____
4. Two cars running into each other _____
5. Fingernails being scratched along the chalkboard _____

REVIEW 1

Write an example of each trope in a complete sentence. You may not use any examples from Review 2.

1. simile _____

2. metaphor _____

3. pun _____

4. personification _____

5. synecdoche _____

6. hyperbole _____

7. onomatopoeia _____

REVIEW 2

Identify the following tropes (simile, metaphor, pun, personification, synecdoche, hyperbole, or onomatopoeia). See if you can identify which selections contain more than one trope.

_____ 1. "Arrow!" said the bowman. "Black arrow! I have saved you to the last. You have never failed me and always I have recovered you."

_____ 2. We await word from the crown.

_____ 3. It was like a globe with a thousand facets.

_____ 4. It shone like silver in the firelight, like water in the sun, like snow under the stars, like rain upon the Moon!

_____ 5. My teeth are swords, my claws spears, the shock of my tail a thunderbolt, my wings a hurricane, and my breath death!

_____ 6. "I have always understood," said Bilbo in a frightened squeak, "that dragons are softer underneath."

_____ 7. He had a famished and a savage look like a dog that has been chained and forgotten in a kennel for a week.

_____ 8. But now the light in Gollum's eyes had become a green fire, and it was coming swiftly.

_____ 9. Tropes are everywhere!

_____ 10. The hiss was close behind him. He turned now and saw Gollum's eyes like small green lamps coming up the slope.

LESSON 22

ALLITERATION

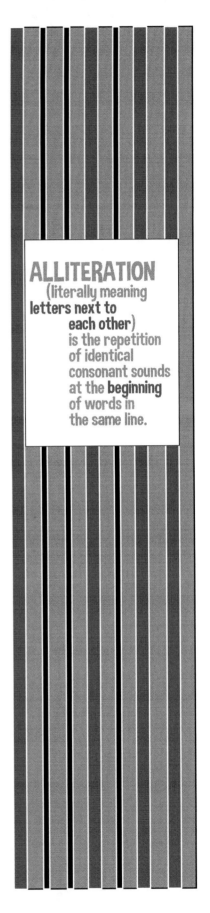

ALLITERATION (literally meaning **letters next to each other**) is the repetition of identical consonant sounds at the **beginning** of words in the same line.

The earliest English poetry did not employ what we would call rhyme at all; instead, it had a unique type of rhyme called alliteration. *Alliteration* (literally meaning letters next to each other) is the repetition of identical consonant sounds at the beginning of words in the same line.

One common form of alliteration that you may be familiar with is the tongue twister.

EXAMPLE

Peter Piper picked a peck of pickled peppers.

PRACTICE

Underline the recurring consonant sounds in the following lines.

1.
Excerpt From PIERS PLOWMAN
By William Langland

In a summer season, when soft was the sun,

I shope me in shroudes, as I a sheep were.

2.
Excerpt From THE RAVEN
By Edgar Allen Poe

Whether tempter sent, or whether tempest tossed thee here ashore,

Desolate yet all undaunted, on this desert land enchanted,

In this home by Horror haunted, tell me truly, I implore.

3.
She sells sea shells by the seashore.

4.
Excerpt From WINTER 72
By Alexander Pope

Fields ever fresh and groves ever green

5.
Excerpt From BEOWULF

Glory great was given to Beowulf.

6.
Excerpt From BEOWULF

Hrothgar's home he had hunted full often.

7.
—Unknown
Conquered by confusing quests,   The doves drift down to dine.

8.
Excerpt From **DOLORES** By A. C. Swinburne
The lilies and languors of virtue   And the raptures and roses of vice.

9.
Excerpt From **LOVE'S LABOUR'S LOST** By William Shakespeare
The preyful princess pierced and prickt a pretty pleasing pricket.

10.
Excerpt From **NEPHELIDIA** By A.C. Swinburne

From the depth of the dreamy decline of the dawn through
    a notable nimbus of nebulous noonshine,
Pallid and pink as the palm of the flag-flower that
    flickers with fear of the flies as they float.

PRACTICE

Choose one of the following tongue twisters to practice and recite individually or in a group.

THE TREE TOAD

A tree toad loved a she-toad

Who lived up in a tree.

He was a two-toed tree toad

But a three-toed toad was she.

The two-toed tree toad tried to win

The three-toed she-toad's heart,

For the two-toed tree toad loved the ground

That the three-toed tree toad trod.

But the two-toed tree toad tried in vain.

He couldn't please her whim.

From her tree toad bower

With her three-toed power

The she-toad vetoed him.

PETER PIPER

Peter Piper picked a peck of pickled peppers.

A peck of pickled peppers Peter Piper picked.

If Peter Piper picked a peck of pickled peppers,

Where's the peck of pickled peppers Peter Piper picked?

SEA SHELLS

She sells sea shells on the seashore;

The shells that she sells are sea shells I'm sure.

So if she sells sea shells on the seashore,

I'm sure that the shells are seashore shells.

MOSES

Moses supposes his toes are roses,

but Moses supposes erroneously,

for nobody's toes are posies of roses,

as Moses supposes his toes to be.

MR. SEE & MR. SOAR

Mr. See owned a saw.

And Mr. Soar owned a seesaw.

Now See's saw sawed Soar's seesaw

Before Soar saw See,

Which made Soar sore.

Had Soar seen See's saw

Before See sawed Soar's seesaw,

See's saw would not have sawed

Soar's seesaw.

So See's saw sawed Soar's seesaw.

But it was sad to see Soar so sore

Just because See's saw sawed

Soar's seesaw!

BETTY BOTTER

Betty Botter had some butter,

"But," she said, "this butter's bitter.

If I bake this bitter butter,

it would make my batter bitter.

But a bit of better butter

that would make my batter better."

So she bought a bit of butter,

better than her bitter butter,

and she baked it in her batter,

and the batter was not bitter.

So 'twas better Betty Botter

bought a bit of better butter.

ESAU WOOD

Esau Wood sawed wood.

All the wood Esau Wood saw, Esau Wood would saw.

All the wood Wood saw, Esau sought to saw.

One day Esau Wood's wood saw would saw no wood.

So Esau Wood sought a new wood saw.

The new wood saw would saw wood.

Oh, the wood Esau Wood would saw.

Esau sought a saw that would saw wood as no other wood saw would saw.

And Esau found a saw that would saw as no other wood saw would saw.

And Esau Wood sawed wood.

ED NOTT & SAM SHOTT

Ed Nott was shot and Sam Shott was not.

So it is better to be Shott than Nott.

Some say Nott was not shot.

But Shott says he shot Nott.

Either the shot Shott shot at Nott was not shot, or Nott was shot.

If the shot Shott shot shot Nott, Nott was shot.

But if the shot Shott shot shot Shott, the shot was Shott, not Nott.

However, the shot Shott shot shot not Shott but Nott.

So, Ed Nott was shot and that's hot!

Is it not?

(It's not the cough that carries you off; it's the coffin they carry you off in!)

LESSON 23

ALLITERATIVE IMITATION

ACTIVITY 1

Read the following excerpts from the Old English epic of *Beowulf*. As you read, listen for the alliteration and the rhythm that it helps to create. Underline the sound which is repeated in each line.

> **THE RAVAGING OF HEOROT HALL BY THE MONSTER GRENDEL**
>
> When night had fallen, the fiend crept near
>
> To the lofty hall, to learn how the Danes
>
> In Heorot fared, when the feasting was done.
>
> The aethelings all within he saw
>
> 5   Asleep after revel, not recking of danger,
>
> And free from care. The fiend accurst,
>
> Grim and greedy, his grip made ready;
>
> Snatched in their sleep, with savage fury,
>
> Thirty warriors; away he sprang
>
> 10   Proud oh his prey, to repair to his home,
>
> His blood-dripping booty to bring to his lair.
>
> At early dawn, when day-break came,
>
> The vengeance of Grendel was revealed to all;
>
> Their wails after wassail were widely heard,
>
> 15   Their morning-woe. The mighty ruler,
>
> The aetheling brave, sat bowed with grief.

BEOWULF'S FIGHT WITH GRENDEL

Now Grendel came, from his crags of mist

Across the moor; he was curst of God.

The murderous prowler meant to surprise

In the high-built all his human prey.

5   He stalked neath the clouds, till steep before him

To the house of revelry rose in his path,

The gold-hall of heroes, the gaily adorned.

Hrothgar's home he had hunted full often,

But never before had he found to receive him

10   So hardy a hero, such hall-guards there.

Close to the building crept the slayer,

Doomed to misery. The door gave way,

Though fastened with bolts, when his fist fell on it.

Maddened he broke through the breach he had made;

15   Swoln with anger and eager to slay,

The ravening fiend o'er the bright-paved floor

Furious ran, while flashed from his eyes

An ugly glare like embers aglow.

He saw in the hall, all huddled together,

20   The heros asleep. Then laughed in his heart

The hideous fiend; he hoped ere dawn

To sunder body from soul of each;

He looked to appease his lust of blood,

Glut his maw with the men he would slay.

25   But Wyrd had otherwise willed his doom;

Never again should he get a victim

After that night.

ACTIVITY 2

Write an alliterative poem that has the same sort of sound and feel as the excerpts from *Beowulf*.

5

10

15

20

25

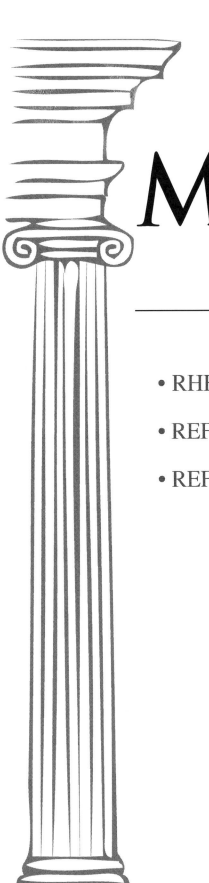

MODULE VIII

- RHETORICAL QUESTION

- REFRAIN

- REFRAINED IMITATION

LESSON 24

RHETORICAL QUESTION

TROPE is a specific figure of speech.

1. SIMILE
2. METAPHOR
3. PUN
4. PERSONIFICATION
5. SYNECDOCHE
6. HYPERBOLE
7. ONOMATOPOEIA

8. RHETORICAL QUESTION
is a figure of speech in which **a question is asked** for some other purpose than obtaining the information requested.

Thus far we have learned about the simile, metaphor, pun, personification, synecdoche, hyperbole and onomatopoeia. The eighth trope that we will cover is the rhetorical question. A *rhetorical question* is a figure of speech in which a question is asked for some other purpose than obtaining the information requested. Often a rhetorical question is used to remind someone of something they already know but do not seem to be considering at the present.

EXAMPLE

Rhetorical Question:

"And just where do you think you're going?"

The expected answer might be:

"No where, Ma'am."

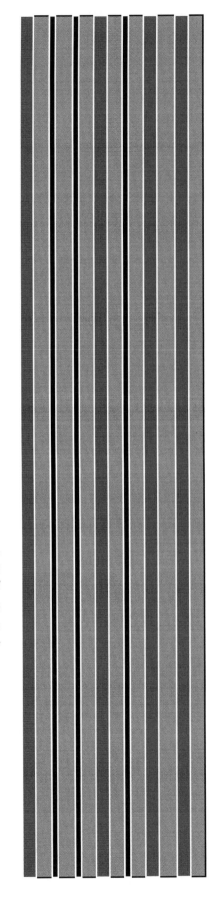

PRACTICE

Write the expected answer to each rhetorical question in the blank. You may have to look up the reference to understand the context of each verse.

_____1. Which of you shall have an ass or an ox fall into a pit, and will not straightway pull him out on the Sabbath day? (Luke 14:5)

_____2. Is not the whole land before thee? (Genesis 13:9)

_____3. Is not Aaron the Levite thy brother, whom I know to be eloquent? (Exodus 4:14)

_____4. Is anything too hard for the Lord? (Genesis 18:14)

_____5. Can any hide himself in secret places that I shall not see him? (Jer. 23:24)

_____6. If God be for us, who can be against us? (Romans 8:31)

_____7. Who shall lay anything to the charge of God's elect? (Romans 8:33)

_____8. Shall mortal man be more just than God? Or shall a man be more pure than his Maker?

_____9. Who shall separate us from the love of Christ? (Romans 8:31-35)

_____10. Where art thou? (Gen. 3:9) _____

ACTIVITY 1

Write three rhetorical questions of your own.

_____

_____

_____

ACTIVITY 2

Underline the rhetorical questions in the following stanzas.

| Excerpt From **A DIALOGUE-ANTHEM** |
by George Herbert

CHRISTIAN:	Alas, poor Death, where is thy glory? Where is thy famous force, thy ancient sting?
DEATH:	Alas poor mortal, void of story, Go spell and read how I have kill'd thy King.
CHRISTIAN:	Poor death! and who was hurt thereby? Thy curse being laid on him, makes thee accurst.

| Excerpt From **COMPLAINING** |
by George Herbert

Art thou all justice, Lord?

Shows not thy word

More attributes? Am I all throat or eye,

To weep or cry?

Have I no parts but those of grief?

REVIEW

Scan the following stanzas.

METER / RHYME SCHEME

Excerpt From **STOPPING BY WOODS ON A SNOWY EVENING**
by Robert Frost

Whose woods these are I think I know.

His house is in the village though,

He will not see me stopping here

To watch his woods fill up with snow.

METER / RHYME SCHEME

Excerpt From **AUTUMN FIRES**
by Robert Louis Stevenson

Sing a song of seasons!

Something bright in all!

Flowers in the summer,

Fires in the fall!

METER / RHYME SCHEME

Excerpt From ESCAPE AT BEDTIME
by Robert Louis Stevenson

The lights from the parlour and kitchen shone out

Through the blinds and the windows and bars;

And high overhead and all moving about,

There were thousands of millions of stars.

METER / RHYME SCHEME

Excerpt From COCKS CROW IN THE MORN
by Mother Goose

The cock doth crow

To let you know,

If you be wise,

'Tis time to rise.

REVIEW 2

Identify the following tropes (simile, metaphor, pun, personification, synecdoche, hyperbole, onomatopoeia, or rhetorical question). See if you can identify which selections contain more than

one trope.

1. _____   "In good sooth," said the King, "his doings have reached even our own royal ears."

2. _____   "Why, how now," quoth the King, wrathfully. "What wouldst thou have me do? Comest thou not to me with a great array of men-at-arms and retainers, and yet art not able to take a single band of lusty knaves without armor on breast, in thine own country! What wouldst thou have me do? Art thou not my sheriff?..."

3. _____   Then the Sheriff turned away with a sore and troubled heart, and sadly he rued his fine show of retainers, for he saw that the King was angry...

4. _____   Then of a sudden it came to him like a flash that were he to proclaim a great shooting-match and offer some grand prize, Robin Hood might be persuaded to come...

5. _____   Then when the Sheriff and his dame had sat down, he bade his herald wind upon his silver horn; who thereupon sounded three blasts that came echoing cheerily back ...

RIDDLE RENDEZVOUS

RIDDLE NO. 17

When first the Marriage Knot was tied

Between my wife and me

My age did hers as far exceed

As three times three does three.

But when ten years and half ten years

We man and wife had been

Her age came up as near to mine

As eight is to sixteen.

Now tell me I pray

What were our ages on our wedding day?

LESSON 25

REFRAIN

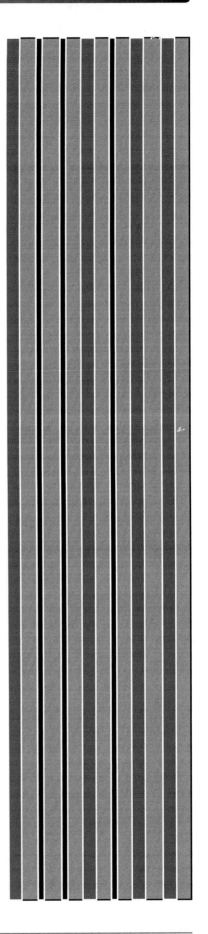

A **REFRAIN**
(in former times
called a burden)
is a line or stanza
which **recurs**
again and again in
a poem.

STANZA
is a paragraph
of poetry.

A *refrain* (in former times called a burden) is a line or stanza which recurs again and again in a poem. It is nothing more than a chorus and is usually found at the ends of stanzas. Poets use refrain to emphasize the meaning of that particular line or stanza which is repeated.

PRACTICE

Underline the refrain in the following stanzas.

THE CHARGE OF THE LIGHT BRIGADE
By Alfred, Lord Tennyson

Half a league, half a league,
   Half a league onward,
All in the valley of Death
   Rode the six hundred.
"Forward, the Light Brigade!
"Charge for the guns!" he said:
Into the valley of Death
   Rode the six hundred.

"Forward, the Light Brigade!"
Was there a man dismay'd?
Not tho' the soldier knew
   Someone had blunder'd:
Theirs not to make reply,
Theirs not to reason why,
Theirs but to do and die:
Into the valley of Death
   Rode the six hundred.

Cannon to right of them,
Cannon to left of them,
Cannon in front of them
   Volley'd and thunder'd;
Storm'd at with shot and shell,
Boldly they rode and well,
Into the jaws of Death,
Into the mouth of Hell
   Rode the six hundred.

Flash'd all their sabres bare,
Flash'd as they turn'd in air,
Sabring the gunners there,
Charging an army, while
   All the world wonder'd:
Plunged in the battery-smoke
Right thro' the line they broke;
Cossack and Russian
Reel'd from the sabre stroke
   Shatter'd and sunder'd.
Then they rode back, but not
   Not the six hundred.

Cannon to right of them,
Cannon to left of them,
Cannon behind them
   Volley'd and thunder'd;
Storm'd at with shot and shell,
While horse and hero fell,
They that had fought so well
Came thro' the jaws of Death
Back from the mouth of Hell,
All that was left of them,
   Left of six hundred.

When can their glory fade?
O the wild charge they made!
   All the world wondered.
Honor the charge they made,
Honor the Light Brigade,
   Noble six hundred.

VIRTUE

By George Herbert

Sweet day, so cool, so calm, so bright,

The bridal of the earth and sky;

The dew shall weep thy fall to night;

      For thou must die.

Sweet rose, whose hue angry and brave

Bids the rash gazer wipe his eye:

Thy root is ever in its grave,

      And thou must die.

Sweet spring, full of sweet days and roses,

A box where sweets compacted lie;

My music show ye have your closes,

      And all must die.

ACTIVITY 1

In the following poem, cross out the refrain, "Lord, Have Mercy on us!" and write your own refrain, keeping the rhyme scheme consistent.

ADIEU, FAREWELL, EARTH'S BLISS
By Thomas Nashe

Adieu, farewell, earth's bliss;

This world uncertain is;

Fond are life's lustful joys;

Death proves them all but toys;

None from his darts can fly;

I am sick, I must die.

      Lord, have mercy on us!

In the following poem, cross out the refrain, "Lord, Have Mercy on us!" and write your own refrain, keeping the rhyme scheme consistent. (continued)

Rich men, trust not in wealth,

Gold cannot buy you health;

Physic himself must fade.

All things to end are made,

The plague full swift goes by;

I am sick, I must die.

        Lord, have mercy on us!

Beauty is but a flower

Which wrinkles will devour;

Brightness falls from the air;

Queens have died young and fair;

Dust hath closed Helen's eye.

I am sick, I must die.

        Lord, have mercy on us!

Strength stoops unto the grave,

Worms feed on Hector's brave;

Swords may not fight with fate,

Earth still holds ope her gate.

"Come, come!" the bells do cry.

I am sick, I must die.

        Lord, have mercy on us!

In the following poem, cross out the refrain, "Lord, Have Mercy on us!" and write your own refrain, keeping the rhyme scheme consistent. (continued)

Wit with his wantonness

Tasteth death's bitterness;

Hell's executioner

Hath no ears for to hear

What vain art can reply.

I am sick, I must die.

        Lord, have mercy on us!

Haste, therefore, each degree,

To welcome destiny;

Heaven is our heritage,

Earth but a player's stage;

Mount we unto the sky.

I am sick, I must die.

        Lord, have mercy on us!

LESSON 26

REFRAINED IMITATION

Scan the following iambic poem; then, write your own using the same meter. Be sure to include a refrain at the end of each stanza.

METER / RHYME SCHEME

—

THE SACRIFICE
by George Herbert

1st Stanza

The Princes of my people make a head

Against their Maker: they do wish me dead,

Who cannot wish, except I give them bread:

Was ever grief like mine?

2nd Stanza

Without me each one, who doth now me brave,

Had to this day been an Egyptian slave.

They use that power against me, which I gave:

Was ever grief like mine?

3rd Stanza

Mine own Apostle, who the bag did bear,

Though he had all I had, did not forbear

To sell me also, and to put me there:

Was ever grief like mine?

In the blanks below, write your own poem using the same meter as Herbert's.

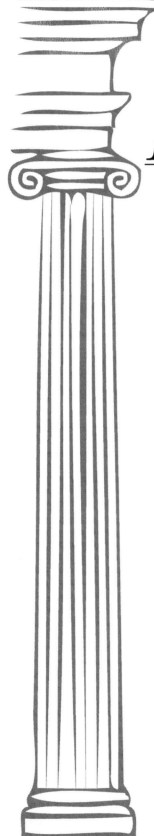

MODULE IX

- OXYMORON

- SPACIAL POETRY

- SPACIAL IMITATION

- EUPHEMISM

LESSON 27

OXYMORON

> **TROPE** is a specific figure of speech.

> 1. SIMILE
> 2. METAPHOR
> 3. PUN
> 4. PERSONIFICATION
> 5. SYNECDOCHE
> 6. HYPERBOLE
> 7. ONOMATOPOEIA
> 8. RHETORICAL QUESTION

> **9. OXYMORON** is a figure of speech in which **two contradictory** words are combined to describe something.

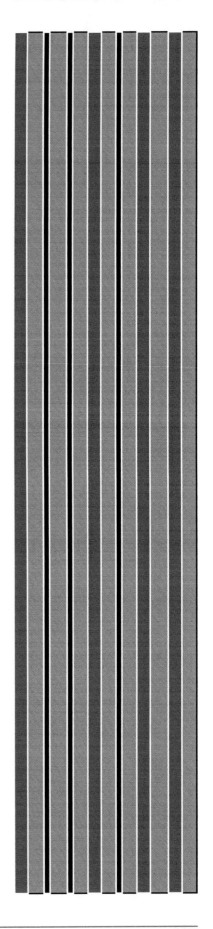

The ninth trope which we will learn is an oxymoron. The word oxymoron comes from two Greek words *oxys* meaning sharp or wise and *moron* meaning foolish. When you combine these ideas, you a have a wise fool.

An *oxymoron* is a figure of speech in which *two contradictory* words are combined to describe something. Poets will often use an oxymoron when they want to communicate something in a unique and striking way.

PRACTICE

Read through the following oxymorons and underline those you have heard before. Just keep in mind they are not all serious.

A little big	Icy hot	Silent alarm
Act naturally	Jumbo shrimp	Social science
Almost exactly	Liquid crystal	Solemn celebration
Alone together	Little Big Horn	Student teacher
American English	Mandatory extra credit	Sure bet
Army intelligence	Middle East peace process	Sweet sorrow
Bitterly happy	Nice cat	Sweet Tarts
Bittersweet	Non-denominational church	Sweet 'n' sour
Bottoms up	Partial consensus	Taped live
Common sense	Passive resistance	Terribly nice
Constant change	Plastic silverware	Terribly pleased
Decent lawyer	Political integrity	Tight slacks
Dress pants	Pretty ugly	Tragic comedy
Exact estimate	Protestant Pope	Unbiased opinion
Freezer burn	(Clement XIV)	Vegetarian meatballs
Fresh frozen	Rap music	Voluntary compliance
Fuzzy logic	Same difference	

ACTIVITY 1

Underline each oxymoron in the following stanzas.

EXAMPLE
Excerpt From **ROMEO & JULIET** by William Shakespeare
Oh <u>heavy lightness</u>! <u>serious vanity</u>!   <u>Mis-shapen chaos</u> of <u>well-seeming forms</u>!   <u>Feather of lead</u>, <u>bright smoke</u>, <u>cold fire</u>, <u>sick health</u>!

Excerpt From **HYMN OF THE NATIVITY** by Richard Crashaw
Welcome, all wonders in one sight!   Eternity shut in a span,   Summer in winter, day in night,   Heaven in earth, and God in man!

The Scriptures have many examples of oxymorons which are very instructive, because God's wisdom is esteemed foolish by man and is yet so wise as to be far beyond man's comprehension.

JOB 22:6
And stripped the naked of their clothing.

ISAIAH 58:10

Thy darkness shall be as the noon day.

MATTHEW 16:25

Whosoever will save his life shall lose it: and whosoever will lose his life for my sake shall find it.

2 CORINTHIANS 6:8-10

As deceivers, and yet true;

As unknown, and yet known;

As dying, and, behold, we live; . . .

As chastened, and not killed;

As sorrowful, yet always rejoicing;

As poor, yet making many rich;

As having nothing, and yet possessing all things.

2 CORINTHIANS 12:10

When I am weak, then am I strong.

1 TIMOTHY 5:6

She that liveth in pleasure is dead while she liveth.

REVIEW 1

Scan the following poems.

METER / RHYME SCHEME

Excerpt From a **MOTHER GOOSE** Rhyme

January brings the snow,

Makes our feet and fingers glow.

February brings the rain,

Thaws the frozen lake again.

March brings breezes loud and shrill,

Stirs the dancing daffodil.

METER / RHYME SCHEME

Excerpt From **ESCAPE AT BEDTIME**

By Robert Louis Stevenson

There ne'er were such thousands of leaves on a tree,

Nor of people in church or the Park,

As the crowds of the stars that looked down upon me,

And that glittered and winked in the dark

METER / RHYME SCHEME

Excerpt From **THE ANSWER**
By George Herbert

My comforts drop and melt away like snow:

I shake my head, and all the thoughts and ends,

Which my fierce youth did bandy, fall and flow

Like leaves about me; or like summer friends,

Flies of estates and sun-shine. But to all,

Who think me eager, hot, and undertaking,

But in my prosecutions slack and small;

As a young exhalation, newly waking,

Scorns his first bed of dirt, and means the sky;

But cooling by the way, grows pursy and slow,

And settling to a cloud, doth live and die

In that dark state of tears: to all, that so

Show me, and set me, I have one reply,

Which they that know the rest, know more than I.

REVIEW 2

Identify the following tropes (simile, metaphor, pun, personification, synecdoche, hyperbole, onomatopoeia, rhetorical question, or oxymoron). See if you can identify which selections contain more than one trope.

_____ 1. The firehose belched forth water as the fire hissed and danced.

_____ 2. That huge terrifying dragon was pretty ugly.

_____ 3. Will Stutely was thankful that Robin Hood had saved his neck.

_____ 4. The sprinter bounded toward the finish line like a cougar after a deer.

_____ 5. As a jewel of gold in a swine's snout is a fair woman who is without discretion.

LESSON 28

SPACIAL POETRY

EXAMPLE

I took an ordinary box, As empty as can be,

And hold it tightly near your heart, Because my love's inside.

But please don't ever open it, Just leave the ribbon tied,

I filled it with a special gift, And wrapped it carefully.

WORDS

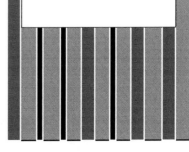

wordsword
...sword
...swo
...rds
...wor
..dsw
 ord
...swo
...rds
...wor
..dswor
dswordswor
.dswordsw
.ordswor
.dswords
.wordswo
.rdsword
.swordsw
.ordswor
.dsword
.wordswo
.rdsword
.swordsw
.ordswor
.dswords
.wordswo
.rdsword
.swordsw.
..ordsw
..ordsw
..ordsw
...ord
...swo
...rd
....s
..

When the shape of a poem corresponds to that poem's content, you have what is called spacial or spatial [spey-shuhl] poetry.

Spacial (also called concrete poetry) poems use the words of the poem to create a visual image that adds to the meaning of the poem. The words and lines are arranged in a way to create an image, a feeling of movement, or even a tension.

ACTIVITY 1

Trace around the perimeter of the poems below with a pencil. What shape is the poem written in?

THE ALTAR
By George Herbert

A broken A L T A R, Lord, thy servant rears,
Made of a heart, and cemented with tears:
Whose parts are as thy hand did frame;
No workman's tool hath touch'd the same.
A HEART alone
Is such a stone,
As nothing but
Thy pow'r doth cut.
Wherefore each part
Of my hard heart
Meets in this frame,
To praise thy name.
That if I chance to hold my peace,
These stones to praise thee may not cease.
O let thy blessed S A C R I F I C E be mine,
And sanctify this A L T A R to be thine.

EASTER WINGS 1 & 2
By George Herbert

Lord, who createdst man in wealth and store
Though foolishly he lost the same,
Decaying more and more,
Till he became
Most poor:
With thee
O let me rise
As larks, harmoniously,
And sing this day thy victories:
Then shall the fall further the flight in me.

My tender age in sorrow did begin:
And still with sicknesses and shame
Thou didst so punish sin,
That I became
Most thin.
With thee
Let me combine,
And feel this day thy victory:
For, if I imp my wing on thine,
Affliction shall advance the flight in me.

ACTIVITY 2

In the space provided, write the following stanzas as spacial poems.

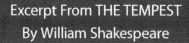

Excerpt From THE TEMPEST
By William Shakespeare

WHERE, the bee sucks, there suck I:

In a cowslip's bell I lie;

There I couch when owls do cry.

On the bat's back I do fly

After summer merrily:

Merrily, merrily, shall I live now,

Under the blossom that hangs on the bough.

Excerpt From RICHES
By William Blake

The countless gold of a merry heart,
The rubies and pearls of a loving eye,
The indolent never can bring to the mart,
Nor the secret hoard up in his treasury

SONG: THE OWL
By Alfred, Lord Tennyson

When cats run home and light is come,
　　And dew is cold upon the ground,
And the far-off stream is dumb,
　　And the whirring sail goes round,
　　And the whirring sail goes round:
　　　　Alone and warming his five wits,
　　　　The white owl in the belfry sits.

When merry milkmaids click the latch,
　　And rarely smells the new-mown hay,
And the cock hath sung beneath the thatch
　　Twice or thrice his roundelay,
　　Twice or thrice his roundelay:
　　　　Alone and warming his five wits,
　　　　The white owl in the belfry sits.

SONG: THE OWL

By Alfred, Lord Tennyson

LESSON 29

SPACIAL IMITATION

EXAMPLE

When
cats run home
and light is come, and
dew is cold upon the ground
and far-off stream is dumb, and the
whirling sail goes round, and the whirling
sail
goes
round; alone and warming his five
wits the white owl in the belfry sits.

ACTIVITY

Choose a shape in which you would like to write a poem. Draw the outline of that shape below, and write a spacial poem that fits inside of it. (Minimum length: _____ lines).

LESSON 30

EUPHEMISM

TROPE is a specific figure of speech.

1. SIMILE
2. METAPHOR
3. PUN
4. PERSONIFICATION
5. SYNECDOCHE
6. HYPERBOLE
7. ONOMATOPOEIA
8. RHETORICAL QUESTION
9. OXYMORON

10. EUPHEMISM is the **substitution** of an agreeable or inoffensive **expression** for one that may offend or suggest something unpleasant.

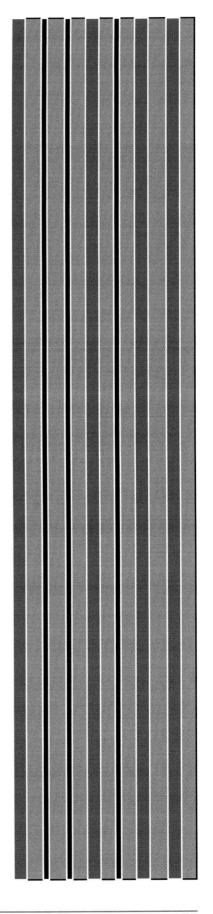

The tenth and final trope that we will learn about is the euphemism. Euphemism comes from two Greek words meaning *good speech*. A *euphemism* is the substitution of an agreeable or inoffensive expression for one that may offend or suggest something unpleasant.

Many euphemisms are used in order to be polite, and they are appropriate. Others are used to cloak sin in inoffensive language so that it seems acceptable or less sinful; this, of course, is inappropriate.

PRACTICE

Circle the euphemisms below that you have heard before. Underline those which you use regularly.

affair	➠	fornification or adultery
heck	➠	hell
remains	➠	corpse, body, stiff
stout	➠	fat
love child	➠	illegitimate child
gosh	➠	God
lavatory, loo	➠	toilet
Thou shall go to thy fathers	➠	die
Our friend Lazarus sleepeth	➠	is dead

ACTIVITY 1

List three of your own euphemisms.

_____

_____

_____

REVIEW

Write the name of the trope next to each definition.

_____ 1. some striking part of an object stands for the whole

_____ 2. making an implicit comparison by calling one thing another

_____ 3. giving human attributes to an inanimate object

_____ 4. a play on words

_____ 5. an extravagant exaggeration

_____ 6. a question asked for a purpose other than obtaining the answer

_____ 7. a substitution for an offensive term

_____ 8. the combination of two contradictory words

_____ 9. a word sounds like what it means

_____ 10. an explicit comparision using _like, as,_ or _than_

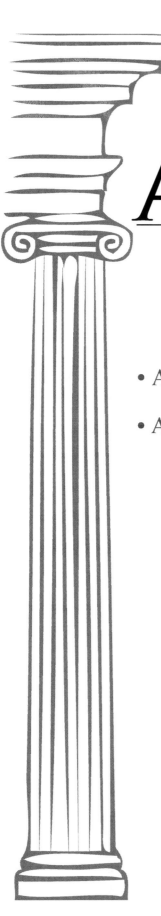

APPENDICES

- APPENDIX A - POETRY ANTHOLOGY
- APPENDIX B - GLOSSARY

APPENDIX A

POETRY ANTHOLOGY

POEMS THAT TELL A STORY (NARRATIVE)

TITLE	AUTHOR
EPICS	
The Epic of Gilgamesh	Anonymous
The Iliad, and The Odyssey	Homer
Aeneid	Virgil (70BC - 19 BC)
The Divine Comedy	Dante Alighieri (1265–1321)
The Canterbury Tales	Geoffrey Chaucer (c.1343-1400)
The Faerie Queene	Edmund Spenser (1552-1599)
OTHER NARRATIVE POEMS	
Sir Patrick Spens.	Anonymous
The Hunting of the Snark	Lewis Carroll (1832 – 1898)
The Rime of the Ancient Mariner	Samuel Taylor Coleridge (1772 – 1834)
Abou Ben Adhem	Leigh Hunt (1784-1859)
The Eve of St. Agnes	John Keats (1795-1821)
Piers Plowman	William Langland (c.1330-1387)
The Nameless Isle	C.S. Lewis (1898 – 1963)
The Song of Hiawatha	Henry Wadsworth Longfellow (1807 – 1882)
The Highwayman	Alfred Noyes (1880-1958)
The Raven	Edgar Allan Poe (1809 – 1849)
My Papa's Waltz	Theodore Roethke (1908-1963)
Ozymandias	Percy Bysshe Shelley (1792-1822)
The Charge of the Light Brigade	Alfred, Lord Tennyson (1809 – 1892)
Lady of Shallot	Alfred, Lord Tennyson (1809 – 1892)
Casey at the Bat	Ernest Lawrence Thayer (1863 - 1940)

POEMS ABOUT NATURE

TITLE	AUTHOR
The Tyge	William Blake (1757-1827)
Nightingales	Robert Bridges (1844 – 1930)
The Donkey	G.K. Chesterton (1874-1936)
The Poplar Field	William Cowper (1731 – 1800)
A Narrow Fellow in the Grass	Emily Dickinson (1820-1886)
The Snow-Storm	Ralph Waldo Emerson (1803-1882)
Stopping by Woods on a Snowy Evening	Robert Frost (1874 – 1963)
Pied Beauty	Gerard Manley Hopkins (1844-1889)
God's Grandeur	Gerard Manley Hopkins (1844-1889)
A Shropshire Lad II: Loveliest of trees, the cherry now	A.E. Housman (1859 – 1936)
Ode to a Nightingale	John Keats (1795-1821)
To Autumn	John Keats (1795-1821)
Trees	Joyce Kilmer (1886 – 1918)
The Maldive Shark	Herman Melville (1819 – 1891)
Ode to the West Wind	Percy Bysshe Shelley (1792-1822)
The Eagle	Alfred, Lord Tennyson (1809-1892)
Fern Hill	Dylan Thomas (1914-1953)
October	Edward Thomas (1878-1917)
A Noiseless Patient Spider	Walt Whitman (1819-1892)
The Lake Isle of Innisfree	William Butler Yeats (1865 – 1939)

POEMS THAT DESCRIBE SOMETHING

TITLE	AUTHOR
The Fish	Elizabeth Bishop (1911 – 1979)
Summer Wind	William Cullen Bryant (1794 – 1878)
The Deserted Village	Oliver Goldsmith(1730-1774)
Snow in the Suburbs	Thomas Hardy (1840-1928)
To Penhurst	Ben Jonson (1572 – 1637)
So This is Nebraska	Ted Kooser
The Swing	Robert Louis Stevenson
The Eagle	Alfred, Lord Tennyson (1809-1892)
The Seasons	James Thomson (1700 – 1748)
Symphony in Yellow	Oscar Wilde

POEMS ABOUT LOVE

TITLE	AUTHOR
To My Dear and Loving Husband	Anne Bradstreet (c.1612-1672)
How do I Love Thee? Let Me Count the Ways	Elizabeth Barrett Browning (1806 –1861)
O, My Love's Like a Red, Red Rose	Robert Burns (1759-1796)
She Walks in Beauty	Lord Byron (1788-1824)
The Good-Morrow and the Sun Rising	John Donne (1572-1631)
Jenny Kissed Me	Leigh Hunt (1784-1859)
Son to Celia: Drink to Me Only with Thine Eyes	Ben Johnson (1572-1637)
To Althea, from Prison	Richard Lovelace (1618-1658)
The Passionate Shepherd to His Love	Christopher Marlowe (1564-1593)
Remember	Christina Rossetti (1830 – 1894)
Sonnet 18: Shall I Compare Thee to a Summer's Day?	William Shakespeare (1564 - 1616)
When You Are Old	William Butler Yeats (1865 – 1939)

POEMS ABOUT HISTORY

TITLE	AUTHOR
ANCIENT HISTORY	
The Destruction of Sennacherib	Lord Byron (1788 – 1824
Kubla Khan	Samuel Taylor Coleridge (1772 – 1834)
Antony and Cleopatra	William Haines Lytle (1826 – 1863)
Overthrow of Belshazzar	Bryan Waller Procter (1787 – 1874)
1400s	
Columbus to Ferdinand	Philip Freneau (1752 – 1832)
Columbus	Joaquin Miller (1837 – 1913)
1500s	
Mary, Queen of Scots	Henry Glassford Bell (1803 – 1874)
Ivry: A Song of the Huguenots	Thomas Babbington Macaulay (1800-1959)
Drake's Drum	Sir Henry Newbolt (1862 - 1938)
John Rogers' Exhortation to his Children	John Rogers (1500 – 1555), From the New England Primer

1600s	
The Landing of the Pilgrim Fathers in New England	Felicia Hemans (1793-1835)
To the Memory of my Beloved, Mr. William Shakespeare	Ben Johnson (1572 – 1637)
On the Lord General Fairfax at the Siege of Colchester	John Milton. (1608–1674)
Of the Late Massacre of Piedmont	John Milton (1608-1674)
Curfew Must Not Ring Tonight	Rose Hartwick Thorpe (1850 – 1939)
First Thanksgiving of All	Nancy Byrd Turner (1880 - 1971)
1700s	
A Poem Sacred to the Memory of Sir Isaac Newton	James Thomson (1700 – 1748)
War for American Independence	
Independence Bell - July 4, 1776	Anonymous
Seventy-Six	William Cullen Bryant (1794 – 1878)
How Sleep the Brave	William Collins (1721-1759)
Concord Hymn	Ralph Waldo Emerson (1803 – 1882)
The Name of Washington	Arthur Gordon Field (1863 - 1923)
Daniel Boone	Arthur Guiterman (1871- 1943)
Betsy's Battle Flag	Minna Irving (1865-1940)
Paul Revere's Ride	Henry Wadsworth Longfellow (1807-1882)
The Siege of Belgrade	Alaric Alexander Watts (1797 - 1864)

French Revolution	
The French Revolution as it Appeared to Enthusiasts at its Commencement	William Wordsworth (1770-1850)
The Burial of Sir John Moore at Corunna	Charles Wolfe (1791 – 1823)
Hohenlinden	Thomas Campbell (1777-1844)
1800s	
The Last Buccaneer (1812)	Thomas Babington Macaulay (1800 – 1859)
On the Departure of Sir Walter Scott from Abbotsford, for Naples	William Wordsworth (1770-1850)
Clipper Ships and Captains (1840-60)	Stephen Vincent Benét (1898 – 1943)
Crimean War (1854-56)	
Charge of the Light Brigade	Alfred, Lord Tennyson (1809 – 1892)
Westward Expansion	
The Kansas Emigrants	John Greenleaf Whittier (1807 – 1892)
Lewis and Clark	Stephen Vincent Benét (1898 – 1943)

War Between the States	
Robert E. Lee	Stephen Vincent Benét (1898 – 1943)
Dixie's Land	Daniel Decatur Emmett (1815 – 1904)
The Blue and the Gray	Francis Miles Finch (1827–1907)
Old Ironsides	Oliver Wendell Holmes (1809 –1894)
The Battle Hymn of the Republic	Julia Ward Howe (1819-1910)
Lines on the Back of a Confederate Note	Major Samuel Alroy Jonas
The High Tide at Gettysburg	Will Henry Thompson (1853 – 1937)
Music in Camp	John Reuben Thompson (1823-1873)
O Captain! My Captain!	Walt Whitman (1819 – 1892)
1900s	
World War I	
Channel Firing	Thomas Hardy (1840-1928)
In Flander's Field	John McCrae (1872 – 1918)
America's Answer — In Flander's Field	R.W. Lilliard
November 1918	Joseph Mills Hanson (b. 1876)
The Trade	Rudyard Kipling (1865 – 1936)

POEMS ABOUT GOD

TITLE	AUTHOR
Once in Royal David's City	Cecil Frances Alexander (1818 – 1895)
Doe the Nexte Thynge	Anonymous
By Night When Others Soundly Slept	Anne Bradstreet (c.1612-1672)
The Shepherd's Song	John Bunyan (1628-1688)
No Scar	Amy Carmichael (1867 - 1951)
O Sacred Head, Now Wounded	Bernard of Clairvaux (1090 – 1153)
Light Shining out of Darkness	William Cowper (1731-1800)
God Moves in a Mysterious Way	William Cowper (1731-1800)
Psalm 23	David (c. 1040–970 BC)
Batter My Heart, Three Person'd God	John Donne (1572-1631)
Death, be not proud	John Donne (1572-1631)
Love bade me welcome	George Herbert (1593-1633)
The Pulley	George Herbert (1593-1633)
Recessional	Rudyard Kipling (1865 - 1936)
O Love That Wilt Not Let Me Go	George Matheson (1842-1906)
When I Consider How My Light is Spent	John Milton (1608-1674)
My Treasure	John Oxenham (1852-1941)
In the Bleak Midwinter	Christina Rossetti (1830-1894)
Immanuel	Charles Haddon Spurgeon (1834-1892)
When I Survey the Wondrous Cross	Isaac Watts (1674-1748)
The Touch of the Master's Hand	Myra Brooks Welch (1877 - 1959)
Thou Hidden Love of God	John Wesley (1703-1791)

POEMS THAT ARE HUMOROUS

TITLE	AUTHOR
Carmen Possum	Anonymous
Matilda: Who Told Lies, and Was Burned to Death	Hilaire Belloc (1870 –1953)
To a Louse	Robert Burns (1759 – 1796)
Jabberwocky	Lewis Carroll (1832 – 1898)
Father William	Lewis Carroll (1832 – 1898)
The Embarrassing Episode of Little Miss Muffet	Guy Wetmore Carryl (1873-1904)
Wine and Water	G.K.Chesterton (1874 –1936)
The Letters at School	Mary Mapes Dodge (1831 – 1905)
Wynken, Blynken, and Nod	Eugene Field (1850-1895)
The Duel	Eugene Field (1850-1895)
Elegy on the Death of a Mad Dog	Oliver Goldsmith (1730-1774)
The Owl Critic	James T. Fields
The Platypus	Oliver Herford (1863-1935)
The Height of the Ridiculous	Oliver Wendell Holmes (1809 –1894)
The Spider and the Fly	Mary Howitt (1799 – 1888)
Hymn to the Belly	Ben Jonson (1572-1637)
The Pobble Who Has No Toes	Edward Lear (1812-1888)
My Shadow	Robert Louis Stevenson (1850 – 1894)
Stella's Birthday March 13, 1719	Jonathan Swift (1667 –1745)

POEMS THAT TEACH

TITLE	AUTHOR
Carmen Possum	Anonymous
England's Sovereigns in Verse	Anonymous
Geography Epitomized	Robert Davidson (1750-1812)
Kings of France	Mary W. Lincoln

APPENDIX B

GLOSSARY

Alliteration ....[uh-lit-uh-**rey**-shuhn]
The repetition of identical consonant sounds at the beginning of the words in the same line

Anapest...........................[**an**-uh-pest]
A metrical foot consisting of three syllables, the first two unaccented and the last accented (◡ ◡ /)

Breve ....[breev, brev]
A mark that shows an unaccented syllable (◡)

Couplet ....[**kuhp**-lit]
A stanza of two lines

Dactyl............................[**dak**-til]
A three syllable metrical foot, the first accented and the second two unaccented (/ ◡ ◡)

Epiphany........................[ih-**pif**-uh-nee]
A showing or revealing.

Euphemism....................[**yoo**-fuh-miz-uhm]
The substitution of an agreeable or inoffensive expression for one that may offend or suggest something unpleasant

Explicit ....[ik-**splis**-it]
Distinctly stated; plain in language; open to the understanding; clear; not obscure or ambiguous

Feet ....[feet]
Combinations of syllables

Full Rhyme.....................[ful rahym]
Two words ending in exact sounding vowels and consonants

Hyperbole......................[hahy-**pur**-buh-lee]
A figure of speech in which an extravagant exaggeration is made in order to add force or intensity to a statement

Iamb ....[**ahy**-am, **ahy**-amb]
Two syllables, the first unaccented and the second accented

Implicit..........................[im-**plis**-it]
Not obvious

Metaphor.....................[**met**-uh-fawr, -fer]
A figure of speech in which one object is being called something which it is not because of a similarity between the two

Meter...........................[**mee**-ter]
The measured rhythm of a line of poetry

Onomatopoeia..............[on-uh-mat-uh-**pee**-uh, -mah-tuh-]
A figure of speech in which words are used that sound like what they mean

Oxymoron.....................[ok-si-**mawr**-on, -**mohr**-]
A figure of speech in which two contradictory words are combined to describe something in a unique and striking way

Personification..............[per-son-uh-fi-**key**-shuhn]
A figure of speech in which a thing or idea is being represented as though it had human qualities or abilities

Poetry...........................[**poh**-i-tree]
A language of pictures and music

Pun...............................[puhn]
A humorous use of words that sound alike or nearly alike but have different meanings

Quatrain........................[**kwo**-treyn]
A stanza with four lines

Refrain..........................[ri-**freyn**]
A line or stanza which recurs repeatedly in a poem

Rhetorical Question......[ri-**tawr**-i-kuhl, -**tor**-] [**kwes**-chuhn]
A trope in which a question is asked for some other purpose than obtaining the information requested

Rhyme...........................[rahym]
A pair of words which begin with different sounds and end with the same sounds

Rhyme Scheme..............[rahym] [skeem]
A combination of letters that represent the rhyming pattern of a poem

Scansion.......................[skan-shuhn]
The process of determining the meter of a poem

Synecdoche .... [si-**nek**-duh-kee]
A trope in which some striking part of an object stands for the whole or the whole for the part.

Simile .... [**sim**-uh-lee]
A comparison of two dissimilar things using the words like, as, or than

Slant Rhyme .... [slant, slahnt] [rahym]
Two words ending in approximate-sounding vowels or consonants

Stanza .... [**stan**-zuh]
A paragraph of poetry

Stress .... [stres]
A mark to show an accented syllable (/)

Triplet .... [**trip**-lit]
A stanza of three lines

Trochee .... [**troh**-kee]
A metrical foot consisting of two syllables, the first accented and the second unaccented.

Trope .... [trohp]
A specific figure of speech

Variable .... [**vair**-ee-uh-buhl]
A letter at the end of a line of poetry to mark the rhyming sound